IMMIGRANTS, EVANGELICALS, AND POLITICS
IN AN ERA OF DEMOGRAPHIC CHANGE

IMMIGRANTS, EVANGELICALS, AND POLITICS IN AN ERA OF DEMOGRAPHIC CHANGE

Janelle S. Wong

Russell Sage Foundation NEW YORK

LIBRARY OF CONGRESS CATALOGING-IN-PUBLICATION DATA

Names: Wong, Janelle, author.
Title: Immigrants, evangelicals, and politics in an era of demographic change / Janelle S. Wong.
Description: New York : Russell Sage Foundation, 2018. | Includes bibliographical references and index.
Identifiers: LCCN 2017051042 (print) | LCCN 2018010286 (ebook) | ISBN 9781610448741 (ebook) | ISBN 9780871548931 (pbk. : alk. paper)
Subjects: LCSH: Evangelicalism—Political aspects—United States. | Evangelicalism—Social aspects—United States. | Conservatism—Religious aspects—United States. | Religious right—United States. | Immigrants—Religious life—United States. | Christianity and politics—United States. | United States—Race relations. | United States—Population.
Classification: LCC BR1642.U5 (ebook) | LCC BR1642.U5 W654 2018 (print) | DDC 320.520973—dc23
LC record available at https://lccn.loc.gov/2017051042

Text design by Matthew T. Avery.

RUSSELL SAGE FOUNDATION
112 East 64th Street,
New York, New York 10065
10 9 8 7 6 5 4 3 2 1

CONTENTS

LIST OF ILLUSTRATIONS

Figures

Tables

ABOUT THE AUTHOR

JANELLE S. WONG is professor of American studies and Asian American studies at the University of Maryland.

ACKNOWLEDGMENTS

This book has been burning on my desk for ten years. Over the course of collecting data and writing, I have moved four times (to Washington, D.C., Los Angeles, Seattle, and back to D.C.), had a second child, and witnessed the election of both Barack Obama and Donald Trump. There are many who have contributed to this project and without them, I would not have started or finished this book.

Jane Iwamura brought me into the world of religious studies, Asian American religions, and the Asian Pacific American Religions Research Initiative where I encountered the awesome Jerry Park, Sharon Suh, David Kim, Joe Cheah, and Khyati Joshi. While I was a faculty member at the University of Southern California (USC), the Religion and Immigration Working Group at the Center for Religion and Civic Culture provided a source of learning, inspiration, and interdisciplinary support. I am grateful to my colleagues in that group, especially Pierrette Hondagneu-Sotelo, Roberto Lint Sagarena, Apichai Shipper, Stephanie Nawyn, and Jane Iwamura. Dara Strolovitch offered encouragement and feedback over many years, and helped me get to the finish line. Karthick Ramakrishnan was a major force toward completion, sharing data, constant energy, and a consistent inquiry ("When are you going to finish your book?"). He has also been there with real and valued friendship. Lorrie Frasure-Yokley, Matt Barreto, Edward Vargas, and Jerry Park made the impossible possible with their collaboration and vision for the 2016 Collaborative Multiracial Post-Election Survey. Jane Junn and Ricardo Ramirez provided intellectual guidance and unwavering support. I am grateful to former colleagues and longtime academic friends, including Viet Nguyen, Marisa Abrajano,

Elizabeth Cohen, Christian Grose, Jennifer Lee, Judith Jackson Fossett, Lisa Garcia Bedolla, Oiyan Poon, and Cynthia Young.

My colleagues at the University of Maryland provided day to day support and gave me the confidence to complete this project. Thank you to Nancy Struna, Julie Greene, Bill Cohen, Christina Hanhardt, Mary Sies, Jason Farman, Psyche Williams-Forson, Jan Padios, Perla Guerrero, Nancy Mirabal, Jo Paoletti, Sangeeta Ray, and La Marr Bruce. Friends in Asian American Studies at the University of Maryland provided friendship and camaraderie. Thank you, Jessica Lee, Grace Lee, Gem Daus, Doug Ishii, Jude Paul Dizon, Kai Kai Mascarenas, and Julie Park.

Algernon Austin and Deepa Iyer inspired me to write and were wonderful writing partners.

My gratitude goes to Rogers Smith, Luis Fraga, John Mollenkopf, George Sanchez, Melvin Oliver, Pei-te Lien, Cathy Cohen, Donald Green, and Michael Jones-Correa. Thank you all for your mentorship and guidance.

Many, including Luis Fraga, Joe Cheah, Pei-te Lien, Michael Jones-Correa, Dina Okamoto, and Erin Chung invited me to give talks to refine and explore the ideas in this book. Jane Junn and Christopher Towler offered essential insights and critical suggestions at important junctures.

Current and former students worked with me to provide critical research assistance for this project: Haven Perez, Matt Jones, Kathy Rim, Jillian Medeiros, Sarah Stohlman, and Adrian Felix conducted interviews. Conor Huynh, Reg Ledesma, Mandy Yu, Kelsey Michael, and Tatiana Benjamin provided research support at the University of Maryland.

I would not have completed this book without Suzanne Nichols, director of publications at the Russell Sage Foundation. She never gave up on this project or on me. Thank you, Suzanne.

Funding for this project was provided by the Russell Sage Foundation, the Woodrow Wilson Center for International Scholars, the USC Center for Law, History, and Culture, and the University of Maryland's Office of Undergraduate Studies.

Thank you to family members Dan and Brenda Wong, Laurel and Henry Eu, Jeff and Teresa Wong, Ellen Greenberger, Mike Burton, and Kari Edwards.

Finally, I am grateful to David Silver for discussing every aspect of this project with me for more than a decade and for filling so many of those days with real friendship and joy.

CHAPTER ONE

IMMIGRATION, RELIGION, AND CONSERVATIVE POLITICS IN THE UNITED STATES

Prior to the election of Republican Donald Trump in November 2016, many political commentators expected the 2016 election results to signal the receding power of white evangelicals in U.S. politics. In the spring of 2015, Chris Kromm anticipated the group's diminishing role in U.S. elections and wrote in the *American Prospect*: "After a period of growth in numbers and political influence in the 1980s and 1990s, white fundamentalist Christians have seen the size of their congregations dwindle, eroding their political clout as well."[1] The executive director of the Public Religion Research Institute, Dr. Robert Jones, made a similar claim in the *Atlantic* in July 2016:

> In recent years, for example, the Southern Baptist Convention, the largest evangelical denomination in the country, has reported steady declines in membership and new baptisms. Since 2007, the number of white evangelical Protestants nationwide has slipped from 22 percent in 2007 to 18 percent today. . . . A look at generational differences demonstrates that this is only the beginnings of a major shift away from a robust white evangelical presence and influence in the country. While white evangelical Protestants constitute roughly three in ten (29 percent) seniors (age 65 and older), they account for only one in ten (10 percent) members of the Millennial generation (age 18–29).[2]

But, to the surprise of many observers, the 2016 election was not the death knell of white evangelicals in American politics. Instead, it signaled the unprecedented consolidation and triumph of white evangelical power in the electoral arena. The results of that election, in which Republican Donald Trump emerged victorious even after bragging on camera about grabbing "pussies," mocking a disabled reporter, and disparaging Mexican Americans, were shocking even to the Trump campaign itself.[3]

Trump won a greater share of white evangelical voters than any Republican nominee in the previous four election cycles, despite a public record of behavior that contradicted "Christian convictions."[4] And even in the face of evidence of their overall demographic decline over the past decade, white evangelicals have maintained a steady presence in the electorate at 26 percent since 2008; in fact, this proportion represents even a slight increase from 2004, when white evangelicals made up 23 percent of all voters.[5] In fact, white evangelicals largely drove the decisive "white vote" for Trump in 2016. Exit polls showed that a majority (57 percent) of white voters supported Trump, but it is worth noting that, if we remove evangelicals from the calculation, analysis of exit poll data shows that a substantial majority of non-evangelical whites supported Hillary Clinton (59 percent). In contrast, a very small proportion of white evangelicals (16 percent) supported Clinton in 2016.[6]

In post-election analyses, pundits turned their attention to rural voters, Rust Belt voters, and disaffected white men, but pondered over the white evangelical vote in particular.[7] Representing more than one in every four voters, and with 81 percent supporting the Republican candidate in 2016 (up from a very solid 78 percent in 2012 and 74 percent in 2008), white evangelicals are undoubtedly among the most powerful voting blocs in U.S. politics today.

Like many Americans, I wanted to better understand the forces driving Donald Trump's win, and, perhaps more importantly, to understand the underlying racial and religious dynamics that led to his victory. As I witnessed the rise of the Trump candidacy and all that it stood for, I asked myself two questions:

First, given major shifts in the racial makeup of the country as a whole and of evangelicals in particular, to what extent is race a central determinant of evangelical political orientations?

Second, if differences across racial groups exist within evangelical America, what accounts for these variations?

I was also interested in the forces that explain and account for the tenacity of the white evangelical political agenda, even in the face of massive demographic change.

These are the primary research questions this project seeks to answer. The project began many years ago as a study of how immigration is changing the U.S. population and its politics. I set out hoping to identify where growing numbers of Latinx and Asian American evangelicals were most likely to exert an impact on the broader evangelical political agenda. As a scholar of immigrant groups, I anticipated that demographic change would fundamentally shake the Christian Right and, perhaps as a result, the very foundations of traditional electoral divides in the United States. However, in the aftermath of an election in which white evangelicals played a pivotal role in electing Donald Trump, I was compelled to adopt a new focus that would incorporate an examination of the limits of demographic change in shaping politics, including evangelical politics, in the United States.

Rising Evangelical Power and Rising Numbers of Immigrants

Although the questions driving this book may be especially relevant to understanding the outcome of the 2016 election and Donald Trump's core constituency (white evangelical voters), they also arise from two long-standing trends that have occurred over my own lifetime and that serve to situate this study. I was born in 1972; since then, the United States has experienced the consequences of the "religio-political earthquake of the 1960s," one of which was a more prominent role for evangelical Christians as a major voting bloc for the Republican Party.[8] Many scholars of religion and politics have observed that at the end of the 1960s attitudes about race and sex were changing sharply and that these transformations "triggered a return to evangelical Protestantism in American political life that hit a high-water mark in the first decade of the 21st Century."[9] Study after study shows a strong association between evangelical identity and conservative political attitudes.[10] Corwin Smidt, for instance, argues that evangelical Protestants constitute a distinct religious tradition in U.S. society because of their unique theological beliefs and worship style, and he further contends that adherents share a set of conservative political beliefs.[11] Clyde Wilcox and Carin Robinson argue that religious orthodoxy helps to explain distinct patterns of political conservatism among evangelicals, and Ted Jelen and Marthe Chandler posit that evangelicals' conservative political attitudes are to some extent a response to messages from elites, such as national leaders, religious media, and pastors.[12] Based on much of the literature on religion and politics, then, evangelical identity is strongly associated with political attitudes owing to shared theological beliefs, cultural commitments, and religious messages.[13] Although some evangelicals align with the political left, scholars of religion and politics observe that the majority are conservative politically; there is no doubt that conservative evangelicals "constitute a key GOP voting bloc in both national and local politics."[14]

At the same time as evangelicals have gained prominence as a virtually unshakable core voting bloc in American politics, I have also witnessed the remarkable demographic transformation of the U.S. population. In 1965, Congress passed the Immigration and Naturalization Act (also known as the Hart-Celler Act), which replaced the provisions of the 1924 Immigrant and Nationality Acts. The earlier immigration laws had established quotas for each sending nation, strongly favored immigrants from northern Europe, and reinforced even earlier restrictions on Asian migration.[15] The Hart-Celler Act ushered in a new era of mass migration to the United States based on skills and family reunification. Because of a confluence of domestic and foreign policy political developments, the 1965 act provided a catalyst for migration from Asia and Latin America.[16] By 2000, 32 percent of adult immigrants were born in Mexico, 16 percent in Central America or the Caribbean, and 27 percent in Asia, while those from Europe made up less than 20 percent of all adult immigrants.[17] Since then, the Asian population in the United States has grown the fastest, followed closely by Latinx, as a result of both migration and births.[18] Migration has changed the face of the United States.[19] According to the Pew Research Center, in 1960 fully 85 percent of Americans identified as "white (non-Hispanic)," a proportion that declined to 63 percent in 2011. In 1960, just 4 percent of Americans identified as Hispanic/Latino and fewer than 1 percent identified as Asian. By 2011, 17 percent of Americans identified as Hispanic/Latino and 5 percent as Asian.[20]

These two post-1965 trends—the rise of evangelicals as a potent political force within the GOP, and massive demographic change driven by international migration—have been studied in parallel, resulting in a large body of work on both topics. However, they have rarely been studied together. For instance, the most highly cited articles on evangelical identity and politics, perhaps because they were published in the 1990s, do not seriously attend to the significant waves of immigration from Asia and Latin America that have occurred in the post-1965 era.[21] Even in later, influential studies on the topic, Latinx evangelicals are either grouped with white evangelicals or undifferentiated from other Latinx.[22] At the same time, the most highly cited research on post-1965 immigration, including research on Asian American and Latinx political participation, mostly fails to attend to evangelical or Protestant Christianity.[23]

To be fair, most scholars of evangelical identity and politics would expect the effects of religion on political attitudes to vary by race and ethnicity. For example, in an essay on "Evangelical and Mainline Protestants at the Turn of the Millennium," Smidt writes that "a growing number of Hispanic and Asian immigrants in this country is coloring evangelical Protestantism in new, and different, ways. . . . Such growing diversity will likely make it more difficult for the tradition to maintain its relatively high levels of issue and voting cohesion politically."[24] Yet the extent and nature of potential variation between these groups and white evangelicals has been neither studied systematically nor treated from a critical perspective.

By examining evangelical identity, post-1965 immigrants, and political attitudes in the pages that follow, I bring two separate political trends and areas of study together. In doing so, I reveal broader themes in U.S. politics, including the unexpected impacts of racial and ethnic variation within traditional voting blocs, and show that demographic change does not always result in a new political order.

Evangelical churches are without a doubt the largest, fastest-growing Asian American and Latinx organizations in the United States, and they are fueling demographic change within the larger evangelical community. The National Hispanic Christian Leadership Conference and the National Latino Evangelical Coalition estimate that there are at least 15,000 Hispanic evangelical congregations in the United States. Templo Calvario, an Assemblies of God church in Santa Ana, California, has a membership of more than ten thousand Spanish-speakers. No fewer than eight thousand Spanish-speakers attend Lakewood Church in Houston every Sunday in the remodeled arena that previously housed the Houston Rockets basketball team. In addition, hundreds of Latinx storefront and home-based churches have transformed religious cityscapes.[25]

A staggering increase in the number of evangelical worshipers within the Asian American community can also be observed in various parts of the country. Korean Central Presbyterian Church, in Centreville, Virginia, boasts forty-six hundred Sunday worshipers, and New Song Community Church in Irvine, California, attracts three thousand Asian American worshipers every Sunday. On many college campuses, evangelical Christian organizations have become predominantly Asian American. Rebecca Kim notes that "there are more than fifty evangelical Christian groups at the University of California (UC) at Berkeley and the University of California at Los Angeles (UCLA)," and that "the percentage of Asian Americans at InterVarsity (a popular campus fellowship organization) chapters on some West Coast and Northeast campuses and throughout parts of the Midwest is often as high as 80 percent."[26] In 2007, reports show, there were as many as seven thousand predominantly Asian American churches nationwide.[27] More recently, mainstream evangelical seminaries have established programs dedicated to Asian American ministries. In 2013, the largest evangelical seminary in the United States, Fuller Seminary, established the Asian American Initiative, a new program dedicated to training students who would "critically and theologically address the issues and concerns of the Asian American community."[28] In fact, between 2009 and 2013, a period when enrollment among whites at evangelical seminaries was declining, Asian American enrollment grew almost 20 percent.[29]

Together, Asian American and Latinx evangelicals constitute about 13 percent of all evangelicals in the United States.[30] This proportion is surely going to increase as new immigrants enter the United States from Asia and Latin America and the number of white evangelicals remains steady or even falls.[31] The Public Religion Research Institute (PRRI) highlighted this demographic trend in its American Values Atlas project, released in 2014:

> Today, roughly two-thirds (66 percent) of Protestants who identify as evangelical or born-again are non-Hispanic whites. Black evangelical Protestants make up 21 percent of all evangelical Protestants

in the U.S., while nearly 1-in-10 (9 percent) are Hispanic. Among evangelical Protestants under the age of 30, only 52 percent are non-Hispanic whites.[32]

Robert Jones, CEO of the Public Religion Research Institute, shows that the proportion of white evangelicals in the population has declined in the past decade, but that the overall proportion of evangelicals in the United States has remained steady.[33] We are now seeing two trends so often studied separately—post-1965 immigration and post-1960 evangelical political consolidation—coming together. This book seeks to better understand the meaning of their relationship in U.S. politics.

The Plan of the Book

At the end of this chapter, I present a short history and demographic overview of evangelical America. Chapter 2 presents a systematic analysis of the role played by race and religion in attitude formation across groups that fall into different racial categories. Here I show that white and nonwhite evangelicals exhibit distinct attitudes about politics, even after accounting for important determinants of political attitudes, such as party identification. In chapter 3, I focus on the drivers of these distinct attitudes among white evangelicals, especially the "boundaries of community" and related feelings of relative discrimination, or what I call "perceived in-group embattlement." This chapter ends by lifting up the voices of evangelicals themselves to narrate their own stories about racial and religious identities and group boundaries. In chapter 4, I take a closer look at how immigration trends are reshaping the evangelical community. I focus on the topic of immigration policy to underscore the main themes in the book and to better understand demographic change and its limits in evangelical America. I conclude by arguing in chapter 5 that although race turns out to matter a great deal in terms of evangelicals' political orientations, there are serious structural limits to the influence of racially diverse evangelicals on the dominant white evangelical agenda. These limits stem from a host of factors, including Asian American and Latinx political participation rates, the fundamentally moderate political positions taken by Latinx and Asian American evangelicals, unequal political mobilization, and the varying boundaries of racial communities. Recognizing these limits, I also identify the points at which evangelicals of color, particularly Latinx and Asian Americans, are likely to exert political pressure in the near future. Although these pressure points do not translate into a dramatic political realignment in the short term, they do reveal the nuanced ways in which demographic change is likely to impact the conservative politics associated with evangelicals in the future.

The Analytic Approach

I used a multimethod approach to answering the questions posed earlier, including systematic analysis of survey data, site visits to evangelical, Pentecostal, and Charismatic churches and religious gatherings, and in-depth interviews. Most of the quantitative data come from the 2016 Collaborative Multiracial Post-Election Survey (CMPS), which includes more than ten thousand completed interviews with white, black, Latinx, and Asian ("Asian American") respondents from December 3, 2016, to February 15, 2017. The survey (and invitation) was available to respondents in English, Spanish, simplified Chinese, traditional Chinese, Korean, and Vietnamese. Details on the survey methodology are included in the appendix.[34] Data were weighted, by racial group, to approximate the adult population in the 2015 American Community Survey (ACS) one-year data file for age, gender, education, nativity, ancestry, and voter registration status.[35] A post-stratification raking algorithm was used to balance each category within plus or minus 1 percent of the ACS estimates. As such, the CMPS provides useful information for making broad and systematic comparisons across racial groups. However, these data do not capture the substantive religious experiences of first- and second-generation immigrants, nor do they reveal the rich context in which immigrant religious adherents come to understand the influence of religion and other factors on their political orientation and participation. Hence, I also move beyond the survey data to better understand how race and religion interact in the everyday lives of evangelical Americans.

For example, from 2006 to 2008, members of my multiracial research team visited more than sixty evangelical and Pentecostal and ten Catholic worship sites to collect data. These site visits add both breadth and depth to the study by providing information not available from the survey on the substantive nature of the relationship between religion and politics for Latinx and Asian American evangelical immigrant Christians—specifically, how religious spaces encourage political participation, share political information, and create political community. The site visits also gave us impressions of the demographic characteristics of members; enabled us to describe the religious leadership, the key themes of the services, rituals, and events, and community-building practices; revealed references made, both explicitly and non-explicitly, to social or political issues; and gave us access to the visual materials available to church and temple members and visitors. At each site, we recorded notes on a standardized "site visit in-take" form that helped us to organize key descriptive information, following Michael Foley and Dean Hoge's method for identifying religious sites for their study *Religion and the New Immigrants*.[36] Some churches and temples were chosen for site visits because we were already familiar with them, and some were chosen because they were mentioned in media stories. Others were chosen either randomly or through word-of-mouth referrals from friends and acquaintances.

In-depth interviews help to inform general findings from the survey analysis and provide a more detailed, descriptive, and process-oriented account of the relationship between religion and politics for evangelical worshipers.[37] I conducted more than seventy interviews with Asian American, Latinx, white, and black worshipers in southern California and Houston, Texas, all of whom were recruited through social and academic networks and through contacts with religious leaders. Unlike the survey interviews, these interviews were not drawn from a national sample. I was able to achieve substantial variation, however, in gender, national origin, occupation, language of interview (English, Spanish, or Korean), and length of residence in the United States. All interviews, which lasted from thirty to ninety minutes, were transcribed in full. All interviewees are listed in table A1.1.

These open-ended, semistructured interviews allowed white, black, Asian American, and Latinx religious adherents to explain and elaborate on their religious beliefs, religious practices, relationships with religious leaders, and racial identity and also to relate the ways in which these aspects of religion and race as well as other potential motivations, concerns, and attitudes informed their political thinking and action. Sample questions included:

"What does the term 'religion' mean to you?"
"What does the term 'politics' mean to you?"
"Do the members of your church/temple ever talk about community problems?"
"Do you ever talk with people at church/temple about moral values?"
"Do you know how your minister/pastor feels about same-sex marriage/affirmative action?"
"How important are the political views of your minister/pastor to your own political views?"
"As a member of both a racial or ethnic community and a religious community, do you ever feel conflict in terms of your views on social or political issues? Why or why not?"

This multimethod approach was invaluable in providing critical data on the relationships and communications between leaders and worshipers, the political and theological content of sermons, the context of services, community-building practices, and the complex racial, religious, and political identities of first- and second-generation immigrant worshipers. Evangelical churches do not focus their mission on political mobilization. Nonetheless, members of these institutions do receive information about the political views of their religious leaders and discuss politics with their fellow members. In interviews, religious adherents were not simply passive recipients of the political information that flowed around them, but often viewed such information with a critical eye.

The History and Context of Post-1965 Evangelical Demography and Politics

Religious categories are dynamic, overlapping, and often contested. Scholarly categories may not mirror categories of self-identification among religious adherents, but the definitions that follow provide a useful point of reference. Scholars of religion and mainstream evangelical organizations describe four theological commitments that together distinguish evangelical Christians: deep reliance on the Bible as the ultimate authority, the sharing of one's faith through missionary actions and other work, conversion through a "born-again" experience, and the belief that Jesus died on the cross to redeem humanity.[38] Evangelicalism also refers to a religious tradition and style of worship.[39] Smidt notes that "within evangelical Protestant churches, one is more likely to encounter contemporary praise services, informal worship styles, and more 'free flowing' services."[40]

As a tradition, evangelical Christianity, being part of the broader tradition of U.S. Christian Protestantism, is deeply rooted in U.S. history.[41] In the 1920s, the divisions between U.S. Protestants that are reflected in current distinctions between "evangelical" and "mainline" Protestants became prominent during the debate surrounding the 1925 "Scopes Monkey Trial." When John Thomas Scopes, a high school science teacher, introduced his students to the theory of evolution, he was charged with violating Tennessee state law. The ensuing trial pitted Christian fundamentalist beliefs against evolutionary theories. William Jennings Bryan, one of the most prominent biblical literalists of the era, and a member of the prosecution's legal team, was widely judged as having failed to defend creationist beliefs and the fundamentalist perspective more generally. As a result of the theological disagreements that arose over the trial, the great majority of fundamentalist Protestants left their churches and denominations and established more theologically conservative houses of worship and organizations. Contemporary evangelicalism grew out of this break.[42] Contemporary mainline Protestants grew out of the "modernist" side of this divide and tend to be less literal in their biblical beliefs, more open to multiple pathways to "salvation," and more focused, when it comes to sharing their faith and changing society, on social structures than on individual conversion.[43]

For several decades after the Scopes trial, evangelical institutions and worshipers remained somewhat marginal to mainstream U.S. social and political life. But they did not stay at the periphery. Scholars trace the rise of evangelicals in U.S. politics to a series of social transformations that began in the 1960s:

> Just as racial tensions peaked in the 1960s and populations shifted from cities and the country to the suburbs, changes in the manufacturing and service sectors of the economy dramatically altered the ways Americans labored. These shifts led to changing roles for

minorities and women in a labor force once dominated by white males. As a consequence of these demographic changes, domestic social concerns displaced previous worries about communism. New issues concerning women's roles in the domestic sphere and the labor force made many Americans uneasy. Further, concerns raised by the sexual revolution, the widespread availability of birth control, and countercultural movements of the 1960s seemed to undermine the very nature of the American family. Unease about race and skyrocketing crime rates in urban areas further contributed to the sense of familial precariousness.[44]

The Republican Party would turn these attitudes to their advantage by "exploiting white anxieties over racial desegregation and concerns about cultural changes affecting the family."[45]

The social characteristics of evangelicals have changed over time. In 1964, just 19 percent of evangelical Protestants (excluding black Protestants) claimed to have attended at least some college. By 2000, this proportion had grown to 45 percent.[46] More recent data from the 2014 Religious Landscapes Survey conducted by Pew show that a majority (56 percent) of evangelicals claim to have attended at least some college.[47]

For some time now, evangelicals have made up about one-quarter of all Americans. In 1964, scholars estimate, evangelicals made up 23 percent of the population.[48] Their proportion increased slightly over time, to 26 percent of the population in 2007, then remained fairly steady (25 percent) into 2014.[49] In contrast to their mainline Protestant counterparts, evangelicals appear to be holding their own in U.S. society. Over the same period of 2007 to 2014, the proportion of mainline Protestants, who made up more than one in four Americans in 1964, declined from 18 percent to 15 percent of the population.[50]

These statistics apply to evangelicals as a whole. If we disaggregate the evangelical population by race, however, it becomes apparent that the white evangelical population is declining. Using General Social Survey (GSS) data from 1988 to 2012 and the Public Religion Research Institute's American Values Atlas (2013–2014), the sociologist Robert Jones shows that white evangelicals made up just over 20 percent of the population in 2008 but had declined to 18 percent of the population by 2014.[51] That evangelicals as a whole have maintained a solid presence in the United States in the face of a slow but steady drop in the proportion of *white* evangelicals can be attributed to growing numbers of *nonwhite* evangelicals.

Latinx and Asian American evangelicals constitute a growing constituency in religious America broadly and in evangelical America in particular. The proportion of Latinx in the United States who identify as evangelical or born-again rose from 12 percent to 16 percent between 2010 and 2013.[52] The proportion of Asian Americans identifying as evangelical or born-again rose from 16 percent in 2008 to about 25 percent in 2012.[53] Nonwhite immigrants seem to be the only source of growth for the American evangelical population.[54] As David Roozen, director of the Hartford Institute for Religion Research at Hartford Seminary, observed in December 2013, "It appears that racial, ethnic and immigrant communities are . . . the pockets of vitality within the overall decline."[55]

The prototypical image of the U.S. "evangelical voter" as white, highly religious, and politically conservative can be traced to the late 1980s, when the frequent references by scholars and political commentators to a "culture war" dividing American voters into two different political camps burnished this image. It was during this time that evangelical voters moved en masse to the Republican Party.[56] These divisions were assumed to be based on different moral and religious orientations.[57] And yet, even as the image of the evangelical voter became more familiar in the American imaginary, some scholars questioned this monolithic representation. For example, Nancy Davis and Robert Robinson wrote in a 1996 article that, "contrary to the portrayal of the religiously orthodox in popular media, and in some recent scholarship, they are not a united conservative front."[58] Davis and Robinson reported, using 1991 GSS data, that evangelicals, even the most orthodox, "are divided on many of today's most contested issues along lines of race, sex, class and age."[59] Many others have also drawn attention to the demographic diversity among evangelical identifiers.[60] Still, the image of the evangelical voter has remained one-dimensional over time.

Immigration from Latin America and Asia may slowly change that image, but it persists, not only in the face of demographic change but also in spite of politically progressive white evangelicals' earnest attempts to counter this monolithic image.[61] The Evangelical Left certainly exists and offers an alternative to the traditional Christian Right ideological framework, but it has not attracted a mass following. Jonathan Merritt, writing in the *Atlantic,* contends, for example, that "a constituency in itself does not a 'movement' make. The latter depends on infrastructure, organization, and leadership, elements that American religious progressives have not been able to produce—despite various attempts—on the scale that the religious right has."[62] I return to an analysis of progressive white evangelicals in the last chapter.

This book questions the assumption that racial and ethnic diversity have a predictable short-term role in disrupting the traditional and conservative Christian base. Observers are indeed correct that Latinx and Asian American evangelical Christians—particularly those who attend church often—tend to be more conservative in their attitudes toward the "hot-button" social issues (such as abortion and same-sex marriage) than do other Latinx and Asian Americans.[63] At the same time, they tend to be more Democratic than their white evangelical counterparts. The fact of the matter is that despite the growing presence of Asian Americans and Latinx in evangelical America, white evangelicals have only become more Republican over time.

The next chapter focuses on the political distinctions between white evangelicals and the growing numbers of nonwhite evangelicals.

CHAPTER TWO

RACIAL DIVIDES IN EVANGELICAL POLITICS

As immigration demographically transforms the evangelical community, a question arises: Do these demographic shifts signal political shifts in evangelical America? One way to examine this question is to compare the political attitudes of white and nonwhite evangelicals. To what extent do the attitudes of these groups converge or diverge?

In this chapter, I attempt to answer this question systematically by using data from a survey that included a large proportion of white, black, Latinx, and Asian American evangelicals. With these data, I can take a close look at both the political commonalities and the political distinctions among evangelicals, comparing not only whites and the growing numbers of Latinx and Asian Americans but also whites, blacks, Latinx, and Asian Americans more generally.

A growing body of research on Latinx evangelicals provides an intriguing start to this inquiry. For example, in a 2007 Pew Research Center report, Luis Lugo and Allison Pond observe that although Latinx evangelicals exhibit the same level of support, or even more support, for conservative positions on same-sex marriage, abortion, and some foreign policy issues, they diverge from white evangelicals when it comes to other policy issues. They note that

> nearly half (47%) oppose the death penalty, compared with just 16% of white evangelicals. A similar, and more predictable, departure from white evangelical attitudes is evident on the issue of immigration. While only a minority (33%) of non-Hispanic evangelicals say that immigrants strengthen American customs and values, a solid majority

of Latino evangelicals hold that view. Latino evangelicals, along with other Latino, also hold generally liberal views on economic issues and are more likely to support government programs and sympathize with poor people than are white evangelicals.[1]

The data analyzed by Lugo and Pond provide initial information about Latinx evangelicals and their political orientations.[2] However, these data are also limited in that they do not place Latinx evangelicals in a multiracial political context. Here I attempt to remedy this limitation through reliance on a study that includes a large sample of Latinx Americans, Asian Americans, black Americans, and white Americans. Previous studies do not allow for such direct comparisons between black, white, Latinx, and Asian American evangelicals using data collected with the same instrument and at the same time.

This chapter is based on analysis of the 2016 Collaborative Multiracial Post-Election Survey.[3] The 2016 CMPS includes more than 10,000 respondents, including 1,032 (self-identified) "Whites"; 3,102 "Black/African Americans"; 3,003 Latinx ("Latino/a"/"Hispanic"), and 3,006 "Asian"/"Asian Americans." The survey was conducted via a "random to web" method: emails were selected randomly from registered voter and commercial vending lists, and individuals associated with those emails were contacted and invited to participate in an online survey.[4] The principal investigators of the CMPS have prepared a full white paper on their methodology.[5] Invitations and surveys were provided in a bilingual format (English, Spanish, Chinese, Korean, or Vietnamese). The response rate was 9.9 percent.

Although the CMPS is not a truly representative sample, the full data are weighted within each racial group to match the adult population in the 2015 ACS one-year data file for age, gender, education, nativity, ancestry, and voter registration status. A post-stratification raking algorithm was used to balance each category within plus or minus 1 percent of the ACS estimates.

Because the census and the Current Population Survey (CPS) do not include questions on religion, it is more useful to compare this sample to other high-quality data with similar populations. Note that the CMPS samples appear to be consistent, for the most part, with other recent survey data.[6] It is also worth noting that "gold standard" surveys such as the American National Election Study (ANES) include a much smaller number of nonwhites and, unlike the CMPS, do not offer the survey in any Asian languages.

There are some important limitations to the CMPS survey data. One of the main questions in the survey utilized here is, "Do you consider yourself an evangelical or born-again Christian?" This question fails to capture the nuances of religious identity and may even exclude some individuals of interest. Further, the CMPS represents a single snapshot of public opinion in the immediate aftermath of the 2016 presidential election cycle. Perhaps the most important limitation of the survey is systematic bias in who opts to take an online survey. However, if we assume that this bias is relatively consistent across racial groups, the CMPS allows us to examine relative differences and similarities across groups, even as we must recognize that it will not allow for the kind of general population estimates associated with a true random sample of the population. Such a sample of Asian Americans and Latinx would be cost- and time-prohibitive. Justin Berry and his colleagues suggest that a listed sample is likely to be more practical than other methods and that it avoids the geographic bias of density samples. Further, they claim that with low-incidence groups such as Asian Americans and Latinx, conventional random digit dial methods do not yield adequate sample sizes.[7] To address concerns over bias related to who opts to take an online survey, I supplement analysis of the 2016 CMPS with data from the 2008 CMPS. That survey collected data via an entirely different methodology: it was telephone only (cell and landline), and the listed sample was built from a multi-state database of registered voters.

Despite its limitations, the 2016 CMPS is quite useful because it provides systematic data on key questions related to the project. One major benefit of the survey for the current study is that it includes questions about respondents' nativity, religious affiliation, political orientations, attitudes toward social issues, and political participation. Further, it represents perhaps the best contemporary multiracial, multilingual survey available that includes large enough numbers of Latinx, Asians, blacks, and whites to allow for meaningful statistical comparisons across both racial and religious groups. Finally, the 2016 CMPS allows for limited (not comprehensive) disaggregation of the Asian American and Latinx samples (Chinese, Vietnamese, Korean, Filipino, Mexican, Puerto Rican, Cuban, and Central American).

Group Profiles: Race and Religion

Before delving into a more thorough examination of whether the association between religion and political attitudes varies by racial category and national-origin group, it is instructive to review some basic descriptive statistics related to religion and socioeconomic status across the major racial categories included in the current analysis.

The proportion of respondents who identify as "born-again" or "evangelical" varies substantially across groups of registered voters in the 2016 CMPS sample. As expected based on past research, born-again identity is most prevalent among black Americans. Nearly half of this group described themselves as born-again Christians (see table 2.1). Whites also demonstrated relatively high rates of evangelical or born-again identity (about one out of every four respondents). At the same time, fully 22 percent of Latinx in the 2016 CMPS sample identified as born-again. Similarly, although Asian Americans are one of the most diverse groups in terms of religious affiliation, 20 percent also described themselves as born-again Christians.

Turning to table 2.2, which presents demographic comparisons among those who identify as born-again or evangelical, we observe that despite their common religious affiliation, white, black, Latinx, and Asian American evangelicals differ in key socioeconomic characteristics and religious behaviors. For example, Asian American born-again Christians were more likely to report having graduated from college than any other group. There is also a substantial income gap between Asian Americans and other groups. Approximately 20 percent of evangelical Asian Americans reported having an annual household income of $100,000 or more, compared to 16 percent of whites and fewer than 10 percent of Latinx and black evangelicals. As expected, more Asian American (81 percent) and Latinx (48 percent) evangelicals indicated that they were foreign-born compared to either white (2 percent) or black (16 percent) evangelicals.

Despite prominent socioeconomic distinctions, born-again survey respondents appear relatively similar in their religious commitment, regardless of racial identity. At least 60 percent of Latinx, Asian American, white, and black evangelicals who took part in the 2016 CMPS said that they attended religious services "almost every" week or

Table 2.1 *Born-Again and Evangelical Identity by Race, Across Three Surveys*

	White	Latinx	Black	Asian American
2016 Collaborative Multiracial Post-Election Survey (N = 10,145)	26%	22%	45%	20%
2012 Pew Asian American Survey (N = 3,511)				25
2014 Pew Religious Landscapes Study (N = 35,071)	29	19	67[a]	

Source: Author's compilation based on 2016 CMPS; Pew Research Center 2012a, 2015.

[a] Includes both those who identify as evangelical and those who identify with a "historically black" church.

"at least every" week. By comparison, fewer than 25 percent of mainline Christians and Catholics attend services that often. Higher attendance at religious services across all racial groups is consistent with other shared evangelical characteristics. Data from the General Social Survey and the Pew Religion and Public Life Project suggest that regardless of racial background, evangelicals are more likely than those affiliated with other religious traditions to believe that the Bible is the ultimate word of God, to believe that their religion is the "one true faith," to pray, and to say that living a religious life is very important to them.[8] Internal group differences among evangelicals in many of these religious beliefs and behaviors can also be observed: evangelical Asian Americans, blacks, and Latinx indicate more religious commitment than their white counterparts.[9]

The Distinct Political Attitudes of White Evangelicals

The 2016 CMPS included a range of political attitude questions, including questions about partisanship, support for candidates in the 2016 presidential race, and ideology. Reporters and academic researchers who study "the evangelical vote" tend to focus on allegiance to the Republican Party and the issues of abortion and same-sex marriage.[10] The CMPS asked similar questions, but also included questions on policy-related items that fall outside of the traditional evangelical agenda: whether immigrants are bad for the economy, feelings on taxing the wealthiest, beliefs about climate change, attitudes toward aid to the poor,

Table 2.2 *Born-Again Identity and Demographic Characteristics, by Race, 2016*

	White *(n = 191)*	*Latinx* *(n = 577)*	*Black* *(n = 1,062)*	*Asian American* *(n = 486)*
Eighteen to thirty-five years old	20%	43%	31%	35%
Foreign-born	2	48	16	81
College graduate	28	14	22	54
High-income ($100,000 per year or more)	16	6	9	20
Homeowner	71	31	37	43
Neighborhood at least 75 percent white (self-reported)	56	22	18	25
Attends religious service or gathering almost or at least every week	62	68	63	83
Place of worship at least 75 percent white (self-reported)	70	38	40	46
Place of worship at least 75 percent black (self-reported)	33	32	71	34
Place of worship at least 75 percent Latinx (self-reported)	32	48	36	34
Place of worship at least 75 percent Asian (self-reported)	34	31	36	55

Source: Author's calculations based on 2016 CMPS.

whether the United States should apologize for slavery, and whether they supported or opposed the Black Lives Matter movement.[11]

Table 2.3 details the bivariate associations between born-again identity and items associated with the traditional evangelical political agenda—such as Republican Party identification, support for Republican candidates and ideology, and belief that there should be a constitutional ban against same-sex marriage—among Latinx, Asian Americans, blacks, and whites who took part in the 2016 CMPS. Two

Table 2.3 *Political Positions of Evangelicals, by Race, 2016*

	White Born-Again (n = 191)	White Other (n = 647)	Black Born-Again (n = 1,062)	Black Other (n = 1,294)	Latinx Born-Again (n = 577)	Latinx Other (n = 1,879)	Asian American Born-Again (n = 486)	Asian American Other (n = 1,884)
Voted for Trump (among registered voters)	75%	54%	7%	4%	31%	15%	37%	20%
Voted for Republican House member (among registered voters)	75	52	7	5	31	21	49	29
Republican Party identification	69	42	8	5	26	18	32	21
Conservative ideology	61	32	21	10	28	16	31	18
Believes that an amendment to the U.S. Constitution to ban same-sex marriages is needed	49	14	37	21	42	16	37	16

Source: Author's calculations based on 2016 CMPS.
Note: Data are weighted.

distinct patterns emerge. First, within each racial category, if we compare those who identified as born-again to those who did not identify as born-again, the former expressed greater levels of Republican
identification and were more likely to have voted for Republicans at
the state level and in the presidential race, to identify as conservative
in ideology, and to support a ban on same-sex marriage. For example,
about 30 percent of Latinx who identified as born-again claimed to
have voted for Republican presidential candidate Donald Trump, but
only 15 percent of non-born-again Latinx said that they voted for him.
Similarly, nearly half of born-again Asian Americans claimed to have
supported a Republican for Congress versus 29 percent of non-born-
again Asian Americans. There are dramatic differences between born-
again and non-born-again Latinx, Asian Americans, and whites across
all of the items in table 2.3. The differences among blacks are much less
stark, though blacks who identified as born-again were more likely to
identify as "conservative" and to support a ban on same-sex marriage
compared to their non-born-again counterparts.

In almost every case, black Americans, born-again or not, tended to be
less conservative than their Latinx, white, and Asian American counterparts. When it came to same-sex marriage, Asian Americans exhibited
similar (relatively low) rates of opposition to same-sex marriage, particularly among those who identified as born-again. This is a bit surprising
given the visible role of Chinese and Korean American Christian pastors in contesting marriage equality.[12] Still, for the most part the data in
table 2.3 mesh well with speculation by scholars and journalists that
evangelical Latinx and Asian Americans represent a rich source of
potential growth for the Republican Party and potential coalition partners with similarly oriented white evangelicals and frequent worshipers.

These data also reveal, however, that variations remain between
white and nonwhite born-again Christians—even on traditional evangelical consensus issues such as voting for Republican candidates, conservative ideology, and party identification. For example, in Republican
Party identification, about eight percentage points separate Latinx
evangelicals and non-evangelicals. A much *larger* spread, about forty
percentage points, separates Republican Party identifiers among Latinx
evangelicals (26 percent) and white evangelicals (69 percent). Similarly,
though a larger proportion of Asian Americans who identify as born-
again voted for Trump compared to non-born-again Asian Americans

Figure 2.1 *Policy Positions of Born-Again Identifiers, by Race, 2016*

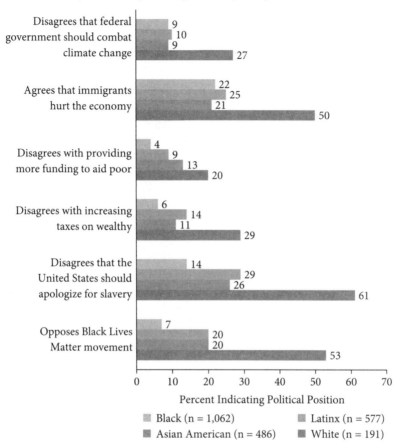

Source: Author's calculations based on 2016 CMPS.
Note: Data are weighted.

(37 versus 20 percent), the difference in Trump support between born-again Asian Americans and born-again whites is much more dramatic (37 versus 75 percent). At the same time, same-sex marriage continues to be more of a consensus policy issue across race within the evangelical community. Note that a robust minority of evangelicals across all groups support a ban on same-sex marriage. On this "hot-button" social issue, there is more convergence across race than between racial groups among those who identify as born-again.[13]

Turning to a broader range of policy issues, we observe that variations between white and nonwhite evangelicals persist. Figure 2.1 shows that on issues ranging from opposition to government intervention to combat climate change to opposition to the Black Lives Matter movement, white evangelicals are almost always at least twice as likely to take a conservative position as their Asian American, Latinx, and black evangelical counterparts. The gaps are least dramatic when it comes to opposition to more government funding to aid the poor. On that policy issue, 20 percent of white evangelicals wanted to decrease government spending on the poor, compared to 13 percent of Asian Americans, 9 percent of Latinx, and 4 percent of black evangelicals. On most other issues, the percentage point gaps between whites and nonwhites are even larger. As noted in the previous chapter, white evangelicals have long been one of the most conservative groups on immigration policy. In the CMPS, the question asked was whether respondents believed that immigrants were bad for the economy in their state. Fully half of all white evangelicals agreed that immigrants were bad for their state economy. Not surprisingly given that a majority of Asian Americans are foreign-born and that Latinx continue to make up the largest groups of immigrants in the United States, fewer than one out of four Asian American and Latinx evangelicals agreed with this statement. Notably, and consistent with past research, black evangelicals were also much more reluctant than their white counterparts to assess the impact of immigrants on the economy as negative.

On issues that might not hit as close to home, such as climate change and taxing the rich, white evangelicals continued to be far more conservative than other evangelicals. Moreover, the gaps between white and nonwhite evangelicals persisted on issues explicitly dealing with race. For instance, while Asian American and Latinx born-again respondents were twice as likely as black born-again respondents to *disagree* that the U.S. Congress should apologize for slavery and to oppose the Black Lives Matter movement, white born-again respondents were four and seven times more likely to take these conservative positions on each of these policies, respectively.

Of course, the 2016 CMPS is a single survey conducted via the Internet. To what extent do these patterns hold if we use another source of data, with a different sample, collected via a different methodology? The 2008 Collaborative Multiracial Political Survey (2008 CMPS) is one such different data source, and it allows us to confirm these findings.

Figures 2.2, 2.3, 2.4, and 2.5 show results from analysis of the 2008 CMPS, the first study of political attitudes and behavior to include

Figure 2.2 *Policy Positions of Latinx Evangelicals and Non-evangelicals, 2008*

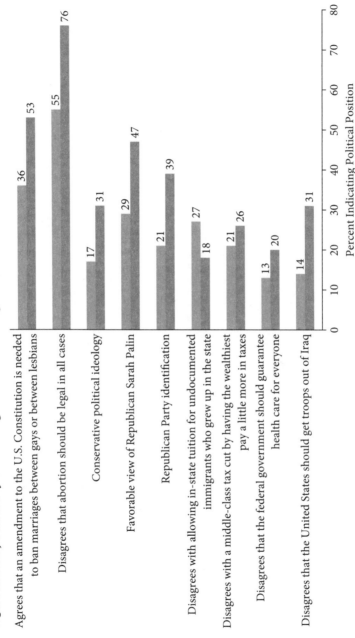

Source: Author's calculations based on 2008 CMPS.
Note: n = 1,577 registered voters contacted by phone.

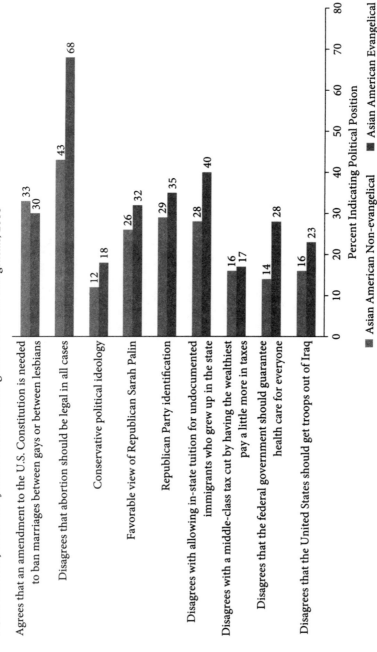

Figure 2.3 *Policy Positions of Asian American Evangelicals and Non-evangelicals, 2008*

Agrees that an amendment to the U.S. Constitution is needed to ban marriages between gays or between lesbians — 33, 30

Disagrees that abortion should be legal in all cases — 43, 68

Conservative political ideology — 12, 18

Favorable view of Republican Sarah Palin — 26, 32

Republican Party identification — 29, 35

Disagrees with allowing in-state tuition for undocumented immigrants who grew up in the state — 28, 40

Disagrees with a middle-class tax cut by having the wealthiest pay a little more in taxes — 16, 17

Disagrees that the federal government should guarantee health care for everyone — 14, 28

Disagrees that the United States should get troops out of Iraq — 16, 23

Percent Indicating Political Position

■ Asian American Non-evangelical   ■ Asian American Evangelical

Source: Author's calculations based on 2008 CMPS.
Note: n = 919 registered voters contacted by phone.

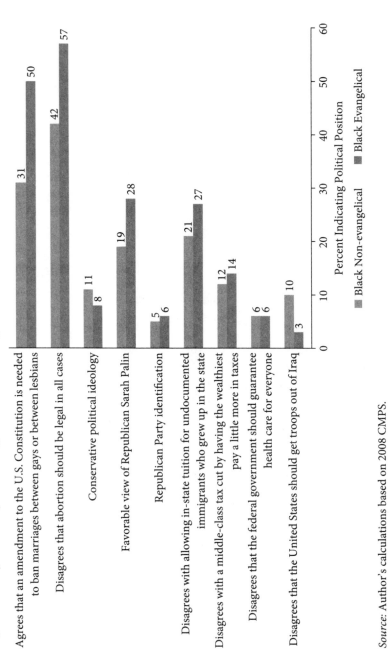

Figure 2.4 *Policy Positions of Black Evangelicals and Non-evangelicals, 2008*

Agrees that an amendment to the U.S. Constitution is needed to ban marriages between gays or between lesbians — 31 / 50

Disagrees that abortion should be legal in all cases — 42 / 57

Conservative political ideology — 11 / 8

Favorable view of Republican Sarah Palin — 19 / 28

Republican Party identification — 5 / 6

Disagrees with allowing in-state tuition for undocumented immigrants who grew up in the state — 21 / 27

Disagrees with a middle-class tax cut by having the wealthiest pay a little more in taxes — 12 / 14

Disagrees that the federal government should guarantee health care for everyone — 6 / 6

Disagrees that the United States should get troops out of Iraq — 10 / 3

Percent Indicating Political Position

■ Black Non-evangelical   ■ Black Evangelical

Source: Author's calculations based on 2008 CMPS.
Note: n = 945 registered voters contacted by phone.

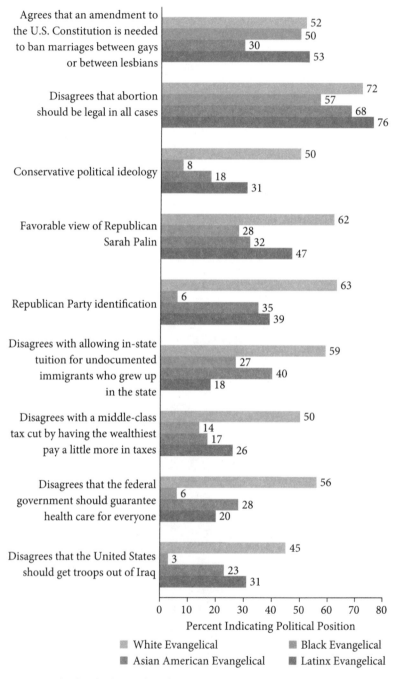

Figure 2.5 *Policy Positions of White Evangelicals and Nonwhite Evangelicals, 2008*

Agrees that an amendment to the U.S. Constitution is needed to ban marriages between gays or between lesbians
52
50
30
53

Disagrees that abortion should be legal in all cases
72
57
68
76

Conservative political ideology
50
8
18
31

Favorable view of Republican Sarah Palin
62
28
32
47

Republican Party identification
63
6
35
39

Disagrees with allowing in-state tuition for undocumented immigrants who grew up in the state
59
27
40
18

Disagrees with a middle-class tax cut by having the wealthiest pay a little more in taxes
50
14
17
26

Disagrees that the federal government should guarantee health care for everyone
56
6
28
20

Disagrees that the United States should get troops out of Iraq
45
3
23
31

0   10   20   30   40   50   60   70   80
Percent Indicating Political Position

■ White Evangelical   ■ Black Evangelical
■ Asian American Evangelical   ■ Latinx Evangelical

Source: Author's calculations based on 2008 CMPS.
Note: Sample of evangelical registered voters contacted by phone: white, n = 319; black, n = 481; Asian American, n = 158; Latinx, n = 293.

robust samples of whites, blacks, Asian Americans, and Latinx in multiple languages (English, Spanish, Mandarin, Cantonese, Korean, and Vietnamese) across multiple states and regions in the United States.[14] The sample included registered voters only, using official statewide databases of registered voters. Importantly, these data were collected via telephone (landline and cell), an entirely different mode from the online survey format of the 2016 CMPS. The 2008 CMPS thus provides a good check on the findings from the 2016 CMPS. If the later findings result from the vagaries of the 2016 CMPS sample (for instance, biases related to who has an email address in the file, or who chooses to take an online survey), the 2008 CMPS, as a product of a different methodology (with its own distinct biases), should not exhibit similar patterns in the association between race and political attitudes among evangelicals.

As it turns out, the results are very similar. Figure 2.2, for example, shows that evangelical Latinx express more conservative attitudes than non-evangelical Latinx on all but one of the issues highlighted (in-state tuition for undocumented students). The percentage point gap is largest on abortion, but in the expected direction almost across the board. The same pattern is found among the 2008 CMPS Asian American sample (figure 2.3). The 2008 CMPS black sample exhibits less conservatism overall, but on traditional evangelical agenda items, the same pattern obtains (figure 2.4). At the same time, the 2008 CMPS confirms the findings associated with the 2016 CMPS. Within each racial group included in the analysis, the general pattern is more conservative attitudes among evangelical members than among those who do not identify as evangelical. However, as figure 2.5 shows, within the evangelical sample, whites hold markedly more conservative political attitudes than their nonwhite counterparts except in attitudes toward abortion restrictions and same-sex marriage.

I conducted a similar analysis with a third data set that included white, black, Latinx, and Asian American respondents but was focused on Asian Americans, hence the title, the 2012 National Asian American Survey.[15] Again, the results are very similar to those found in the 2016 CMPS. Within each racial group in the analysis, evangelicals were more conservative than their non-evangelical coethnics. At the same time, white evangelicals were much more conservative than nonwhite evangelicals in their vote choices, in their position on government-sponsored health care, and in their willingness to tax the wealthy (see table A2.1). In short, with these findings, we can be confident that the results of the CMPS analysis are not unique.

These basic comparisons hint that while evangelical religious affiliation certainly shapes the political orientation of Latinx and Asian Americans, the effects of race may be equally important or even more so. However, before drawing any conclusions about the impact of race on evangelical political attitudes, it's important to ask whether these differences are driven by race or by other covarying influences, such as party identification, socioeconomic status, immigrant status, or factors such as conservative ideology or residence in the U.S. South.

The Persistence of Differences Between White and Nonwhite Evangelicals

Further analysis shows that even after taking into account Republican Party identification, socioeconomic status, immigrant status, and other potential intervening factors, white evangelicals are more conservative than Asian American, black, and Latinx evangelicals on a range of political issues.

I conducted three different analyses—first pooling the white and black born-again respondents, then pooling white and Latinx born-again respondents, and finally pooling white and Asian American born-again respondents. The dependent variables include the policy attitudes highlighted in figure 2.1. Each of the eight policy questions was analyzed separately for each pooled sample (white-black, white-Latinx, and white–Asian American). The control variables included party identification, income, education, age, sex, nativity, frequency of attendance at religious services, conservative attitudes related to trust in the federal government, economic anxiety, and residence in the U.S. South. The key independent variable, racial identity, was captured by dummy variables for "Latinx," "Asian American," and "black," with "white" constituting the excluded category in every model.[16] I employed ordered logit and logit regression models to better isolate the effects of racial identity from the control variables and calculated predicted probabilities associated with taking the conservative position on each policy, and for each racial group, compared to whites. For ease of interpretation, I show the difference between the predicted probabilities of taking the conservative position if the respondent was white versus black, Latinx, or Asian American. Each bar in figure 2.6 shows that calculation—for example, the predicted probability of taking the conservative position on an issue if black *minus* the predicted probability of taking the conservative position on the issue if white (see predicted probabilities for each group in table A2.2). Negative numbers indicate that the predicted probability of taking the conservative position on an issue was larger among whites than the group indicated.

It is clear, then, from the results displayed in figure 2.6 that even when we take into account the effects of partisanship, socioeconomic status, and other potential intervening variables such as economic anxiety or beliefs that the government in Washington can never be trusted, race is still an important predictor of policy attitudes among those who identify as born-again. It should be noted that the differences between whites and other groups are not statistically significant in the analysis of same-sex marriage attitudes. Across all other issues and comparisons, white evangelicals are more likely to take a conservative position on every one of the issues examined, all else being equal.

Some might ask whether the differences between whites and non-whites are driven by forces beyond socioeconomic status or partisanship, such as general conservatism, feelings of economic precarity, or region (such as living in the South). But even when I include variables to capture these potential influences—such as a belief that the federal government can "never" do anything right (a measure of general political conservatism), feelings that the economic conditions in the country are "getting a lot worse" (a measure of economic insecurity), and a variable for whether respondents reside in the southern United States—the same substantive results obtain.

I would emphasize that the patterns I describe here do not obtain only with the 2016 CMPS. I found similar patterns using the 2008 CMPS, the traditional telephone survey.[17] In this earlier study, along with dummy variables for "Latino," "Asian American," and "Black," the equations included variables measuring the interaction between racial category and born-again identity (for example, "Latino x born-again"). Whites were the comparison category. The dependent variables were attitudes related to two broad domestic policies: government-sponsored health care, and taxation of the wealthy to provide a middle-class tax cut. Each of these policy questions was analyzed separately.

Figure 2.6 *Differences in Predicted Probabilities Between White and Nonwhite Born-Again Respondents, 2016*

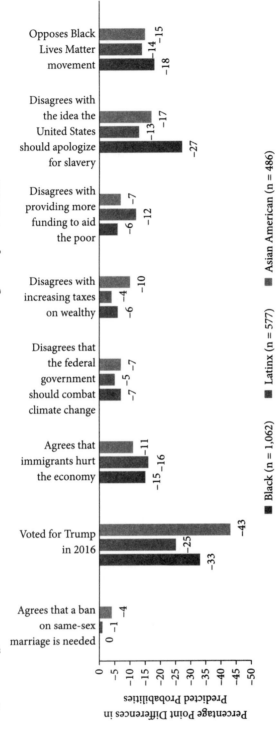

Source: Author's calculations based on 2016 CMPS.

Note: Data are weighted. The figure is based on ordered logit and logit models that include party identification (Republican), age, education, income, female, foreign-born status, frequency of "attendance at religious services or gatherings," general conservatism (beliefs that the federal government can "never" be trusted), economic anxiety (economic conditions in the country are getting "much worse"), and southern residence. Differences between groups on the same-sex marriage item are not significant; differences between Latinx and non-Hispanic white respondents on the climate change and the tax items, and differences between Asian American and white respondents on aid to the poor and the tax items are significant at $p < .10$. All other differences are significant at $p < .05$. Sample size for white, $n = 191$ (excluded category). Sample sizes for the "voted for Trump" question include registered voters only: black, $n = 744$; Latinx, $n = 355$; Asian American, $n = 244$; white, $n = 136$.

The control variables included income, education, age, sex, nativity, party identification, and attendance at religious services. The main effects were captured by dummy variables for racial identity ("White" is the excluded category) and born-again identity.

Perhaps most important for the current investigation is that this additional analysis also shows that the effects of born-again identity are likely to depend on race. The main effects for race and the inter- action terms for black identity and Latinx identity with born-again identity in the model of government-sponsored health care were both statistically significant. In the model of redistributive tax policy ("dis- agrees with a middle-class tax cut by having the wealthiest pay a lit- tle more in taxes"), the main effects for race and all three interaction variables between racial identity and born-again identity were also statistically significant. The results reported in figure 2.7 help to illus- trate more clearly the effects of born-again identity on attitudes toward government-sponsored health care and redistributive tax policies across racial groups. The effect sizes associated with being born-again (relative to non-born-again members of the same racial group) on atti- tudes toward these two policies are much larger among whites than among blacks, Latinx, or Asian Americans. In the case of redistributive tax policy, for example, the effect size associated with being born-again is at least seven times larger for whites than for any other group. This is additional evidence that the effects of race on evangelical political atti- tudes are not simply a matter of differences in socioeconomic status or even partisan loyalties across racial groups, because even when these differences are accounted for, we see that the effects of evangelical iden- tity depend a great deal on race.

Intragroup Differences

Like all "racial" groups, the terms "Asian American" and "Latinx" rep- resent broad, socially constructed categories. Understanding the diver- sity *within* these panethnic social categories has been a critical scholarly endeavor.[18] The data in figures 2.8 and 2.9 focus on distinct national- origin groups within the "Latinx" and "Asian American" catego- ries, including three Latinx groups (Mexican, Cuban, and Central American) and four Asian American groups (Chinese, Indian, Korean, and Filipino). Because this analysis focuses on those members of Asian

Figure 2.7 *Size of Effect on Two Policy Positions Associated with Evangelical Identity Relative to Positions of Non-evangelical Members of Same Racial Group, 2008*

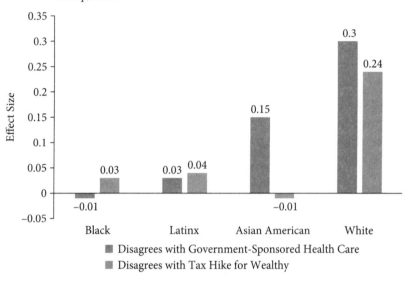

Source: Author's calculations based on 2008 CMPS.
Note: Disagrees with government-sponsored health care analysis, n = 3,136; disagrees with tax hike for wealthy analysis, n = 3,106.

American or Latinx national-origin groups who identify as born-again, the sample sizes for some of these groups are relatively small (see the figures for sample sizes). As such, we might expect to see less consistency in the findings related to specific national-origin groups. For the most part, however, the figures show the same general pattern established in the previous analysis of panethnic groups. That is, with little exception, these national-origin groups appear less conservative than their white counterparts, even after we account for party identification and other potential intervening influences with regression analysis. The key patterns observed thus far are likely to hold among national-origin subgroups *within* the broader Asian American and Latinx populations. Again, some of the sample sizes are quite small (see table A2.3), so caution must be exercised in putting forth these conclusions. Nevertheless, the distinctions between these groups and white evangelicals are apparent.

There are two points worthy of emphasis here. First, when we think about "the evangelical vote," we must attend to race. And in doing so, we

Figure 2.8 *Differences in Predicted Probabilities Between White Evangelicals and Evangelicals from Three Latinx National-Origin Subgroups, 2016*

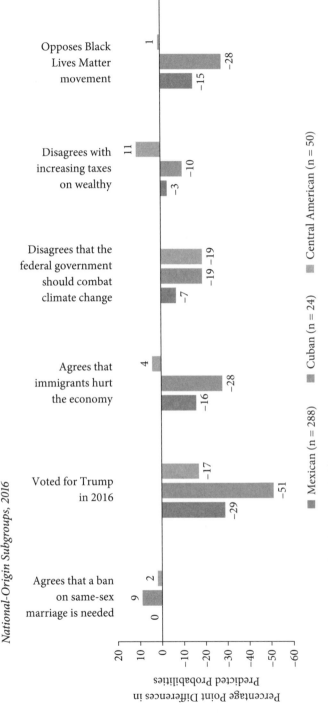

Source: Author's calculations based on 2016 CMPS.
Note: Data are weighted. The figure is based on ordered logit and logit models that include party identification (Republican), age, education, income, female, foreign-born status, and "attendance at religious services or gatherings." Sample size for white, n = 191 (excluded category). Sample sizes for the "voted for Trump" question include registered voters only: Mexican American, n = 163; Cuban, n = 16; Central American, n = 33; white, n = 136.

Figure 2.9 *Differences in Predicted Probabilities Between White Evangelicals and Evangelicals from Four Asian American National-Origin Subgroups, 2016*

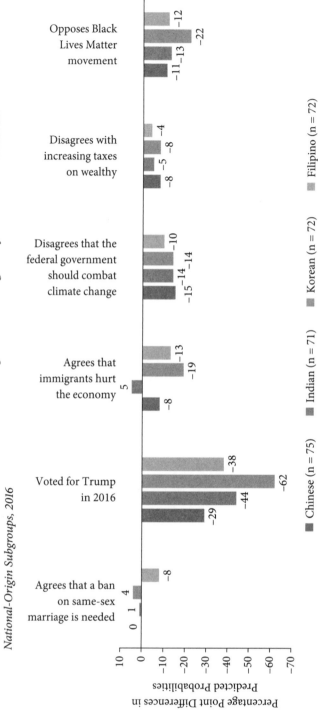

Source: Author's calculations based on 2016 CMPS.

Note: Data are weighted. The figure is based on ordered logit and logit models that include party identification (Republican), age, education, income, female, foreign-born status, and "attendance at religious services or gatherings." Sample size for white, n = 191 (excluded category). Sample sizes for the "voted for Trump" question include registered voters only: Chinese, n = 144; Indian, n = 23; Korean, n = 34; Filipino, n = 72. Sample sizes for the "voted for Trump" question include registered voters only: Chinese, n = 144; Indian, n = 23; Korean, n = 34; Filipino, n = 18; white, n = 136.

are likely to see a real divide between white and nonwhite evangelicals. Second, there are important variations in the degree to which different nonwhite groups exhibit support for particular political candidates or issues. We see, for instance, that not only are black evangelicals more progressive on most issues than Latinx or Asian American evangelicals, but there are some differences in the degree to which members of subgroups, such as Chinese, Indian, Mexican, or Central American, support or oppose various issues. Despite the intragroup variation seen in figures 2.8 and 2.9, no Latinx or Asian American evangelical subgroup seems as conservative across the board as white evangelicals, nor does any such subgroup appear to be more conservative than whites. Elsewhere, I did an even deeper dive with an Asian American sample.[19] I include these analyses of Asian American and Latinx subgroups to highlight the fact that although "Asian American" and "Latinx" are socially constructed categories—as are "whites" and "blacks"—in the United States these categories capture important social and political distinctions. The distinction between whites and nonwhites in particular does not disappear when we break out national-origin groups within the larger Asian American or Latinx categories.

Of course, whites are not a monolithic group either.[20] I also examined whether these consistent and broad conservative political attitudes maintain among subgroups of white evangelicals. Whites from the South are more likely to exhibit the most conservative attitudes, as are those over the age of thirty-five. Notably, there are still instances when the overall patterns described in this chapter hold even if the analysis is conducted only with respondents from outside the South or respondents younger than thirty-five.

Conclusion: Race Matters in Evangelical Politics

In this chapter, I have shown that much of the variation in the political attitudes of evangelicals centers on race. Religious identity certainly matters for understanding political attitudes, but my findings also underscore that racial identity may shape political attitudes among people who share evangelical faith—even beyond the traditional black-white binary.[21] To this point, we see that by some measures, nonwhite evangelicals display greater levels of religiosity than white evangelicals, but hold political attitudes very different from those of white evangelicals.

For example, according to a 2012 Pew survey, Asian American evangelicals (72 percent) are more likely than white evangelicals (49 percent) to say that their religion is the "one, true faith leading to eternal life," and they are more likely than their white counterparts to attend religious services on a weekly basis (76 versus 64 percent).[22] However, Asian American evangelicals also express more liberal political attitudes than white evangelicals.

Asian American and Latinx evangelicals are generally more open to the Republican Party, more ideologically conservative, and more likely to vote for a Republican candidate than other members of their racial and ethnic communities. So, although Latinx and Asian American born-again Christians are not "natural" Republicans, as I have demonstrated, it is also true that they may not fit easily within the traditional civil rights coalition and may be unmoved by the conventional appeals to minorities used by secular ethnic advocacy groups.

This chapter's demonstration that both race and religion shape the political attitudes and behavior of Asian American and Latinx evangelicals contributes to our understanding of "the evangelical vote," but we must also recognize that, despite the significance of faith, race clearly remains an enduring force in U.S. politics. What remains less clear is what drives these general differences between white and non-white evangelicals, and whether these differences will change the dominant direction of evangelical politics in the future. These themes are explored in the next chapters.

CHAPTER THREE

COMMUNITY BOUNDARIES AND PERCEPTIONS OF IN-GROUP EMBATTLEMENT: THE MECHANISMS DRIVING VARIATIONS IN POLITICAL ATTITUDES AMONG EVANGELICALS

Though there are important exceptions, white evangelicals, more than any other group in America, express a deep anxiety about potential threats to the traditional boundaries of their national community. This anxiety manifests in a nostalgia for a period in American history when blacks and other nonwhites were considered either outside the bounds of the American national community or peripheral to it; Robert Jones has vividly described this community as "White Christian America."[1] In her research on evangelical identity and political partisanship in the United States and Canada, the sociologist Lydia Bean advances two important arguments that help to explain why evangelicals with similar theological and moral commitments align politically with the ideological right in the United States but not in Canada.[2] Even if one can question the dichotomy that Bean sets up between the development of white evangelical identity in each country, her theorizing is useful for understanding potential distinctions between white and nonwhite evangelicals in the United States.[3]

Bean begins by arguing that in the United States, (white) evangelical identity and partisanship have become deeply entwined. For the white evangelicals in her study, voting Republican was an expression of religious identity.[4] Religious identity and partisanship were tightly fused among white U.S. evangelicals as a result of lay leaders in evangelical churches professing the United States to be a "Christian nation" under siege by Democrats, liberal elected officials, and progressive advocacy organizations. Thus, "Christian identity was defined in opposition to liberals, understood as both a religious and political category."[5] In Canada, Bean argues, being a "true Christian" and being a "true Canadian" are defined in nonpartisan terms.[6] In the second step of her argument, Bean contends that white evangelical churches in both the United States and Canada engage in "religious constructions of national identity" that matter for policy attitudes, particularly antipoverty policy. Yet there are critical distinctions between U.S. and Canadian evangelicals in how they conceptualize the members of their national community. In Canada, Bean writes, redistributive social programs are framed "as an expression of national solidarity, in ways that [extend] cultural membership to poor people." In contrast, U.S. churches frame antipoverty programs and outreach to the poor as "expressions of 'grace' toward morally unworthy people."[7] In other words, for white evangelicals in the United States, "the poor" stand outside the boundaries of their religious national community.

Bean's work focuses on white evangelicals. I argue that, like their Canadian counterparts, nonwhite evangelicals in the United States hold a more expansive notion of the "national community" than do white evangelical Americans. Here it is instructive to define what I mean by a "national community." A national community is the group bounded by a broad sense of who the "we" consists of when individuals ask themselves who "we" are as a nation. It is a sense of collective identity and belonging within the nation-state. I follow, to a large extent, Bean's work here, but apply it to a different context. The white evangelical Americans in Bean's study commonly drew a set of boundaries between "us" and "them." In particular, U.S. white evangelicals viewed their community not only as religious (conservative Christians), but also as political (political conservatives). They cultivated a sense of religious Christian nationalism that not only drew boundaries between "believers" and "nonbelievers" but also connected religious community to "those who want to restore our nation to its glorious past by overcoming liberal influences in politics."[8] Hence, the boundaries of national community for U.S. white evangelicals were created by fostering a sense of collective identity that tightly linked those who shared not only a religious identity but also a political viewpoint.

Importantly, how an individual defines out-groups helps to create a sense of shared national community. For example, in Bean's study, discussions were not explicitly about politics, but individuals were encouraged to think about their community boundaries in ways that "put Christians on one side of the line, and groups associated with the Democratic Party on the other."[9] I extend this argument to assert that there are important variations in how evangelicals in the United States conceptualize the boundaries of "national community." In particular, I argue that nonwhite evangelicals are likely to define "national community" and an associated sense of "who we are" in ways that extend beyond Christian identity to include coethnics and others who have faced systematic discrimination by the state. Nonwhite evangelicals might prioritize the election of a Christian president and the "restoration of a Christian nation," but for them the boundaries of national community are also likely to encompass non-evangelical coethnics, particularly other people of color.

Several other scholars have developed theories of boundary-making around religious identity that may be useful here. For example, Elizabeth Theiss-Morse, in her work on U.S. nationalism, contends that those with a strong national identity

> define their national group more narrowly than weak identifiers, setting strict boundaries on who is included in the group and who is excluded. They are also more likely to marginalize group members who aren't prototypical. Marginalized group members are less likely to be helped and less likely to be listened to when they raise concerns about the national group.[10]

Again, the sense of "who we are" is what matters here. Theiss-Morse makes clear that there are variations within any group in who is considered prototypical and who is considered marginal. Although it is obvious that group boundaries "demarcate who is included or excluded from the group," Theiss-Morse writes, "boundaries are also important to intragroup dynamics."[11] Why is this the case? As Theiss-Morse explains, in-group members who do not reinforce the prototypical image associated with the group "are potentially threatening to the group because they make the group appear less exclusive and less distinctive . . . they muddy the group boundaries and that raises questions about the group's viability."[12]

Although Theiss-Morse is most interested in nationalism, her work on intragroup variation is critical here. She draws on social identity theory to emphasize group variations *within* a particular identity category.[13] Prototypical members of the group, she argues, are much more likely to be accepted and helped by the group than marginalized members. This is borne out by research in social psychology.[14] In the current case, prototypical members of the evangelical community are white. Nonwhite status is not typical of the U.S. evangelical community, and thus nonwhite evangelicals might be considered more marginal in terms of group identity boundaries. Theiss-Morse suggests that they would still be accepted within the group, but because nonwhite evangelicals do not clearly embody the group's norms and they blur the group's boundaries, they occupy a more marginal position within the group. To build on these ideas, I forward the argument that the differences in their sense of group boundaries and belonging as a result of their prototypical (white) or marginal (nonwhite) status within the evangelical community lead white and nonwhite evangelicals to exhibit different political attitudes.

Further, data from the 2016 CMPS provide some evidence that white and nonwhite evangelicals exhibit different perceptions of national belonging. The survey included three questions that bear on a sense of belonging:

"How strongly do you feel like you belong in the United States?"
"How much do you feel like an outsider in the United States?"
"How often do you think that other people try to exclude you from
    U.S. society?"

Their answers to these three questions revealed a greater tendency among nonwhite evangelicals, compared with white evangelicals, to not feel a strong sense of national belonging, to feel more excluded, and to feel like outsiders (table 3.1).

Boundary-drawing and distinct conceptions of "who we are" may be one driving force behind racial differences in political attitudes among evangelicals. I find support for this thesis in the qualitative interviews conducted for this project.

Table 3.1 *Evangelicals' Sense of Belonging, by Race, 2016*

	White (n = 191)	Black (n = 1,062)	Latinx (n = 577)	Asian American (n = 486)
"How strongly do you feel like you belong in the United States?" (percentage answering "slightly" or "not at all")	3%	9%	13%	15%
"How much do you feel like an outsider in the United States?" (percentage answering "moderately" or "strongly")	13	26	23	31
"How often do you think that other people try to exclude you from U.S. society?" (percentage answering "always" or "very often")	8	25	20	15

Source: Author's calculations based on 2016 CMPS.
Note: Data are weighted.

The Broader Boundaries of National Community Among Asian American and Latinx Evangelicals

The white evangelicals interviewed for this project connected their religious identity to their political identity. Sandra, a twenty-five-year-old white woman who attended an evangelical church in Simi Valley, California, said that she identified with the Republican Party because "they tend to be against abortion. They tend to believe [in] marriage between a man and a woman." Republicans, she said, "will tend to uphold a lot of the same beliefs" that she held herself. A forty-one-year-old white man who attended a Pentecostal church in Agua Dulce, California, said, "What was most important to me [about voting in the past election] is to have a president that has Biblical moral values. I'm a registered Republican. . . . I only vote Republican because usually the candidate . . . supports the things that I also support that are based on the Bible, based on what God says. That's how I make my decisions."

Some white evangelical Christians did not identify with the Republican Party. For example, one twenty-six-year-old man who attended a Pentecostal church in Bellflower, California, claimed that, "as far as the official platform of the parties, I don't know that any of them would represent my values." He also noted that, because he was one of the few members of his church in favor of same-sex marriage, he avoided discussing politics at his place of worship. For the most part, however, the white evangelicals we interviewed claimed that their conservative political viewpoints were a reflection of their religious and Bible-based beliefs.

The scholars cited here would argue that these conservative political viewpoints are deeply rooted in white evangelicals' sense that the policies of Republican candidates reinforce the boundaries of their national community. For white evangelicals in the United States, this sense of community excludes not only those who support abortion or same-sex marriage but also proponents of "big government." Bean, for example, would argue that white evangelicals tend to believe that redistributive economic and social policies threaten religious identity and especially the role of Christians in the public square. They blame the growth of government programs on the "decline in the public role of Christianity" in American life. In the past, they contend, the church was the primary social welfare institution, but today it is the government.[15] Christian nationalism, then, excludes those who might take advantage of these social programs, such as the poor and people of color. And unlike white evangelical culture in Canada, Bean contends, white evangelical culture in the United States discourages cross-cutting identities that might decouple evangelical identity from the Republican Party platform.[16]

Christian identity is critical to nonwhite evangelicals too, but the interviews revealed that they have a sense of national community that extends to other people of color and immigrants. For members of evangelical nonwhite immigrant groups in the United States, both race and religion remain critical aspects of identity, and hence, for them, national community boundaries are associated with those identities. Not surprisingly, the Asian American and Latinx evangelicals interviewed for this project discussed the impact of both their racial and religious identities on their attitudes about politics. For instance, a twenty-eight-year-old second-generation Filipina who lived in southern California and attended a Pentecostal church described the tension between these two identities in the political realm: "When I was in college, a lot of those issues mixed up a lot because I was Filipino American, and a lot of the Filipino Americans at UCLA are involved politically with a lot of really liberal groups, and a lot of these groups did not agree with the Christian faith at all. So, at that time, I felt a lot of conflict." Similarly, a first-generation Korean American woman who lived in Texas discussed how her membership in ethnic and religious communities affected her party identification: "I always see myself as very conservative, so Republican, I would say, . . . on the values side. But some of the things that they're doing on Social Security or immigration, for me, I always see myself as a working-class immigrant, so in that sense it's more Democratic Party. So I don't know. It's a tough call."

These remarks hint that multiple identities related to religion and race may simultaneously shape the boundaries of national community and associated political attitudes of Asian American and Latinx evangelicals. For example, in a Spanish-language interview (translated), a Latina immigrant in Houston who attended Lakewood Church did not hesitate to say that belonging to a religious community was of the utmost importance to her. In another Spanish-language interview, a Mexican immigrant in her forties, who described herself as both Catholic and born-again, noted that her religious community was a fundamental part of her life.

INTERVIEWER: How important is it to belong to a church or a religious community?

INTERVIEWEE: I think it is important. The word of God says that we should surrender.

INTERVIEWER: [If] it's from one to ten, like . . .

INTERVIEWEE: Oh, ten.

When she was asked about the importance of being part of the Mexican American community, however, her answer was less emphatic.

INTERVIEWEE: Well, it's not that important. Just the act of you being Mexican should not influence you to solely be Mexican or identify [yourself] with them. The importance is that you have those values, that you always conserve them, and that your kids conserve them.

INTERVIEWER: Yes. From one to ten, how important is it for you to be part of a Latin community, ten being the most important, as always?

INTERVIEWEE: I think a seven.

Annabel, a Chinese woman in her late thirties who attended an evangelical church in Irvine, California, saw traditional Chinese folk beliefs as possibly problematic because they do not stem from the Christian God. She mentioned that many Chinese immigrants in the United States grew up with superstitions and refer to the lunar calendar and the Chinese zodiac. She saw that as "a problem or issue" because she did not "think that's from God."

Even those with a very strong sense of racial or ethnic community consistently emphasized the importance of their spiritual identity and the critical role of spiritual community in their lives. A Korean American man who attended a nondenominational evangelical church in Santa Monica, California, explained that a sense of community was the cornerstone of his spiritual life. He remarked, "I can't be alone on my island just worshiping God." He also noted that he believed that his Christian life could be viewed as a triangle, with God at the top, himself as an individual worshiper on one side, and other people on a third side. In his words, "We're called to fellowship with other believers as well. So just sharing worship together, things like that." At the same time, he discussed his racial and ethnic identity with seriousness, noting that he had been to Korea several times and that contact with his Korean relatives was a distinguishing feature of his life experience. Yet in his reflections about Korean American identity and Christian identity, he also claimed that his spiritual identity "outweighed" his cultural identity: "Well, I do identify with the Korean American community, and would actually label myself as an American Korean, so I would put the 'American' first, with a Korean background. However, my Christian identity is way more important to me than my Korean identity."

Leyla, a forty-year-old Chinese American woman who attended a pan–Asian American church in the Houston suburbs, echoed these comments: "I sometimes struggle with doing the right—you know, putting myself Christian first and then Chinese second. I know sometimes there's a tension there. My Asian upbringing tells me one thing, and sometimes it is opposite of what the Christian says. But ultimately, I strive for being Christian first and Asian second."

Charles, a second-generation Japanese American, suggested that race was an important part of his identity, a feeling that connected him to other nonwhite groups.

> Oh, gosh, for me, I'm really fascinated about racial identity. Especially being, I guess—what would you call it? A marginal person. It's like a sociological term where you're part of two cultures but not a part of either, especially as an Asian, because no matter how long I stay here, how much I assimilate American values and American traditions, my face will always pass me out as someone who does not belong. And I feel really kind of passionate about the Asian American experience in particular. Also, growing up in West Covina, which is predominantly Latino, I think that's a huge part of my experience as well. The black experience in the past three years has become a huge part of my life, because that's the community I'm in, that's the world that I'm in. So it's huge to me. I talk about it all the time.

At the same time, for Charles, spiritual identity was at the "core" of his identity. He considered his relationship with Christ to be "preeminent" and read the Bible in the morning, prayed throughout the day, and stayed in dialogue with God throughout the day.

A Guatemalan immigrant who attended an evangelical church in Los Angeles also described her Christian identity as central. She said that it infused her relationship with her family, her coworkers, and "everything, because the Bible teaches us that we have to do everything with love and the main point is love."

Not one of the nonwhite interviewees who identified as born-again or evangelical described their ethnic or racial identity as having primacy over their spiritual identity, and yet they all freely discussed race and racism. For instance, it is clear that the evangelical worshipers quoted here felt a strong sense of connection with their faith communities, but also that the boundaries of their Latinx and Asian American communities extended beyond their religious communities to encompass other people of color. Such a broader sense of national community leads to more support for programs that might benefit members of that community.

Almost every interviewee also emphasized the importance of electing a "Christian president" and said that their Christian values were strongly associated with their political values. For example, when Annabel, the Chinese American woman from Irvine, was asked about her past voting choices, she argued that she voted for George Bush in 2000 mostly "because he is a man of God. . . . I may not agree with him 100 percent, but at least he fears God. That's sufficient." A Colombian immigrant man, age forty-five, who attended a mostly white Pentecostal church in southern California said that the Republican Party did a better job than the Democratic Party of representing his values because "they're more on the Christian values that I hold dear." He added that "the candidates that I've followed and I've respected have been usually from the Republican Party and they've been Christian."

Although they share a similar commitment to a Christian religious community and see their religious identity as being important to their political values, nonwhite evangelicals differ from their white evangelical counterparts in that they recognize and reflect upon a nonwhite identity and feel a connection to a nonwhite community. This may help to explain their more moderate political positions on many issues compared with white evangelicals, such as universal health care and government provision of social services. Their interests are driven in large part by their religious identity, but also tempered in part by their connections with their racial or ethnic community, which they see as distinct from their spiritual community and as perhaps having distinct political interests.

Joseph, an eighty-one-year-old Mexican American man who was born in Kemp, Texas, attended an Assembly of God church growing up, and identified as born-again, described a very strong religious influence on his political views. He claimed that he supported the Republican candidate for president because "I, as a Christian, I believe what the Bible teaches," and the Democratic candidate "was against what the Bible and the Lord God teaches." Joseph's primary political concerns were "homosexuality, abortion and those things that are contrary to what I believe the Bible says about it." Joseph expressed many views consistent with those of his white evangelical counterparts. For example, he adamantly relied on religious scripture to support his political positions. Yet he also described a racialized childhood that his white evangelical counterparts would not have experienced firsthand: "I'm an old man. I've gone through many years where I or my race, Hispanics, we were low-class supposedly, and we were more impoverished than the so-called white people. We had lower jobs, less pay. We were part of that."

Joseph was a strong Republican in part because of his belief that Republicans share his positions on abortion and same-sex marriage. By contrast, another study participant, a sixty-year-old Puerto Rican man named Luis, who attended a multiracial evangelical church just outside of Los Angeles in Wilmington, California, supported the Democratic Party, even though he shared Joseph's conservative positions on abortion and same-sex marriage. On these issues, Luis said, "I just have to follow what the Bible tells me and pray for those people, because that's what Jesus says." He supported the Democratic Party because he believed that it is more committed to "helping people." Luis noted that his pastor spoke out against abortion and same-sex marriage, but also against racial discrimination, which Luis said he had experienced himself growing up. Like others interviewed for this study, Luis expressed a mix of conservative and progressive viewpoints that can partly be explained by the convergence of spiritual and racial identities.

Creighton, a black man who worked as an optician in Simi Valley and attended the same church as Sandra, the young white evangelical woman described earlier, also reflected on his racial identity in describing his background. "I'm a fifty-two-year-old black man. I grew up in Compton, California. Race will always be an issue. We can't hide from it. We can't run from it." Leyla, the Chinese American woman who attended a pan–Asian American church in Houston and said that she sometimes felt tension between her Christian identity and her Asian identity, nevertheless still felt a connection to the Asian American community because her parents were Taiwanese immigrants and because she grew up in both a Chinese American neighborhood and a predominantly Chinese American church.

Felipe, a Mexican immigrant who identified as born-again, provides a final example of how evangelical Latinx and Asian Americans navigate race and religion when it comes to politics. Now sixty-eight, Felipe immigrated to the United States from Mexico City when he was eighteen years old. He arrived at Long Beach, California, on his own and found work as a custodian at a local high school. He attended an Assemblies of God Pentecostal church of about 1,500 people and was a founding member of the Spanish-language service there. Felipe grew up in a Catholic household, but his grandfather was Pentecostal and introduced Felipe to evangelical Christianity. Felipe had a conversion experience in October 1992. He had been drinking heavily for most of that year, and one Friday night he had a moment of self-reflection:

> I prepared another drink, and I felt like I was alone, and I asked myself, *Why am I alone?* And then I answered myself: *I've been alone most of my life.* Because I left my house when I was fifteen years old. When I came here, I said, I've been alone all my life, why it is that I feel alone now? And then I said, I know what I'm gonna do. I'm gonna put my drink in the refrigerator and I'm gonna go to church. So that's what I did.

Felipe went to a local church and stepped into the sanctuary, where a group was singing and praying. The pastor gave a sermon and then invited attendees to approach the stage for the late-night prayer service. Felipe's plan was to walk to the stage and then walk out of the church while the others were praying so they would not see him leave.

> I'm gonna walk out and nobody is gonna see me leaving, so I'm gonna leave. So I went to the front, to the platform, the pulpit. And something happened right there, because the minute I—first I was thinking of leaving right away, but then I remember that I said, *Well, God, I don't know how to pray, but I just know that I'm a sinner. Forgive me.* So I said that. I started crying. I leave my hands up and I started crying. It was, like, nine o'clock at night. I was crying and crying and asking for forgiveness. I wanted to stop crying, but I couldn't. And every time I would lift my hands, I felt something, like something was coming from heaven and was still in the air. I was shaking and sweating and crying. And then, when I put my hands down to the floor, I felt electricity running. For a second I thought to myself, *Maybe the pastor has some electric wires so whenever somebody touches it, it starts shaking.* But before I knew it, it was already one o'clock. I know that people started getting up and wanted to go home, but they cannot go home because I was there praying and crying most of the time.

After that night, Felipe stopped drinking and smoking, and he moved to a different neighborhood. He became a regular churchgoer. He described himself as deeply spiritual as opposed to "religious." For Felipe and many others, religion had to do with the formal rituals and performance of Christianity, while spirituality was about one's personal relationship with Jesus and connection to God, outside of the rituals and rules of any particular denomination or religious institution.

Felipe then described how his spiritual values influenced his vote choice in 2000, when he voted for George W. Bush because Bush, he felt, was a "Christian and believed in God" and so would do the right thing. However, he began to question that choice when the Bush administration initiated an invasion of Iraq. Felipe opposed the war in Iraq. He also began to question other policies, including what he described as Republicans' lack of concern for the poor. Felipe had come to feel split about the two parties, despite his continued and deep Christian identity. He supported Social Security expansion and believed that the government has a strong role to play in providing social services to marginalized groups. He was also concerned with Latinx political empowerment: "I believe that we Latinos make a difference in this nation. So it matters to me to be part of a Latino community, because we have, from being Latinos, being nobody, we came to be somebody. I believe we've been helping this nation to become what it is . . . and to me, being part of that in the Latino community, to make a difference where we live . . . here in the U.S., to me it's very important."

Felipe's story may help explain why Asian and Latinx evangelicals hold both strong conservative views on issues like abortion and same-sex marriage and more moderate views on other issues, particularly those related to the role of government in everyday life. Their connection to a nonwhite community affects their conception of the role of government and policies that might affect people of color, and this perspective influences their general political outlook, even as they hold other, more conservative views.

White evangelicals also discussed race in the interviews, and they uniformly condemned racial discrimination in society. With these interviewees, however, discussions about race were not always comfortable or invited. For instance, a fifty-three-year-old white evangelical man who attended a predominantly white, nondenominational evangelical church in southern California said that he thought about race only "because I'm forced to." He said, "I don't believe there is such a thing as racial equality or inequality. There are just races, and they are what they are. We're forced to think of things in racial terms. I certainly have no reason to believe that's anything that God necessarily wants, for us to think in terms of white, black, brown, Asian, whatever. . . . I think there's an overemphasis on racial issues. For me, race itself is not an issue." Another evangelical white man, who attended a Pentecostal church in Simi Valley, expressed a more conservative view on racial equality. He described the biblical teachings on racial equality:

> In my understanding, what the Bible teaches about equality is that in terms of racial equality, your social equality is less important than your relationship to God and your role in the Kingdom of Heaven. So, I think the Bible says we're all equal, but if you find yourself in an unequal situation due to politics, society, or whatever, prioritize your identity as a Christian over your identity as an inferior member of society. So, I think that means something, it's not revolt and rebel against your masters, but Paul's point is, don't revolt and rebel, but be good and be the best slave you can be. . . . Racial equality I think is less important to the Bible than your relationship to God.

Other white evangelicals said that discussions about racial inequality in their churches were simply "not a priority." In churches that were majority-nonwhite or explicitly multiethnic, racial identity and racial inequality were not frequently discussed, though sometimes these topics were addressed in a Sunday sermon. It is clear that the non-white and white interviewees thought about race and belonging in very different ways.

Perceived In-group Embattlement

White evangelicals' strong commitment to enforcing national boundaries seems to be buttressed by a sense of embattled Christian nationalism among them.[17] Fully 59 percent of white evangelicals believe that the United States used to be a Christian nation, but is no longer.[18] This proportion has increased over time. In 2012, 48 percent of white evangelicals expressed this view. White evangelicals are also the religious group most likely to believe that "the American way of life needs protection." Further, nearly 80 percent of white evangelicals contend that "discrimination against Christians is now as big a problem as discrimination against other groups in America." This statistic is striking even compared to other white Christian groups. Just about 55 percent of white mainline Protestants and white Catholics believe that discrimination against Christians rivals discrimination against other groups.

In a 2016 study, Robert Jones and his colleagues show that nostalgia for the society of the 1950s is more prominent among white evangelicals than any other group in the United States.[19] For example, while strong majorities of Latinx Catholics (64 percent) and black Protestants (69 percent) believe that the "American culture and way of life" have mostly improved since the 1950s, a majority of white evangelicals say that the American culture and way of life have worsened since that time. This nostalgia is accompanied by deep unease about racial equality and demographic change. According to Jones and his colleagues, white evangelicals (68 percent) are much more likely than whites as a whole (57 percent) to believe that "today discrimination against whites has become as big a problem as discrimination against blacks and other minorities."[20]

The political scientists Christopher Parker and Matt Barreto suggest that a flip side to this nostalgic mind-set is a fear that newcomers and new attitudes will erode the dominant culture in the United States.[21] In their thorough treatment of the attitudes of Americans who express support for the Tea Party, Parker and Barreto argue that their support for the group's agenda is likely rooted in anxiety over progressive forces that "threaten to steal 'their' country."[22] Tea Party support is tied to supporters' belief that their vision of America is threatened by liberal organizations and leadership. Similarly, the sociologist Algernon Austin, in his book examining the 25 million Americans who have expressed the most disdain and antipathy toward the first black president of the United States, Barack Obama, contends that the rise of the so-called Obama-Haters cannot be explained by party identification or ideological conservatism alone.[23] Rather, the most important correlates of intense hatred for Obama are not only antiblack attitudes but negative attitudes toward a host of "multicultural elements" in U.S. society, including Muslims and immigrants.

Data from the 2016 CMPS align with these trends. Table 3.2 shows that when assessing the levels of discrimination faced by different groups in society, white evangelicals reported higher levels of discrimination toward whites compared with the degree to which nonwhite evangelicals assessed discrimination against whites. In contrast,

Table 3.2 *Evangelicals' Perceptions of Discrimination Faced by Different Groups, by Race, 2016*

	White (n = 191)	Black (n = 1,062)	Latinx (n = 577)	Asian American (n = 486)
Whites face "a lot" of or "some" discrimination	43%	19%	16%	20%
Muslims face "a lot" of or "some" discrimination	70	83	81	72
Blacks face "a lot" of or "some" discrimination	60	91	76	67
Latinos face "a lot" of or "some" discrimination	55	74	73	55
Asian Americans face "a lot" of or "some" discrimination	34	56	43	58
Immigrants face "a lot" of or "some" discrimination	64	82	81	70

Source: Author's calculations based on 2016 CMPS.
Note: Data are weighted.

when it came to assessing levels of discrimination against various "out-groups" in society, white evangelicals were less likely than nonwhites to believe that these groups face discrimination. For example, 43 percent of white evangelicals believed that whites face "a lot" of or "some" discrimination compared to 17 percent of black, 16 percent of Latinx, and 20 percent of Asian American evangelicals who believed that whites face this level of discrimination. The proportion of white evangelicals who rated the levels of discrimination faced by other racial groups, "immigrants," and "Muslims" as "a lot" or "some" was consistently lower than the proportion of black and Latinx evangelicals who rated the discrimination faced by those groups as "a lot" or "high." Asian American evangelicals were more moderate in their assessments of group discrimination, but still more likely than their white counterparts to claim that it is out-groups that face discrimination. Of course, it is critical to acknowledge here that these out-groups are not mutually exclusive. One can be "Muslim" and "black" or "white" and an "immigrant."

Table 3.3 *Relative Differences Among White and Nonwhite Evangelicals in Perceived Discrimination (Compared to Perceptions of Discrimination Against Whites), 2016*

	White	Black	Latinx	Asian American
Difference between discrimination against whites and discrimination against Muslims	−27%	−64%	−65%	−52%
Difference between discrimination against whites and discrimination against blacks	−17	−72	−60	−47
Difference between discrimination against whites and discrimination against [respondent's group]	0	−72	−57	−38
Difference between discrimination against whites and discrimination against immigrants	−21	−63	−65	−50

Source: Author's calculations based on 2016 CMPS.
Note: Data are weighted.

Turning to table 3.3, we see the distinct ways in which white and nonwhite evangelicals assessed the *relative difference* in discrimination faced by whites versus different out-groups. These results show that white evangelicals consistently perceived the levels of discrimination between whites and the out-groups listed in the table as less different in relative terms than did other groups. Table 3.3 attempts to measure what I call "perceived in-group embattlement" among the white evangelicals in the CMPS study. This key measure is a variable that captures the extent to which respondents believed that their own racial group faced discrimination *compared* to the extent to which "Muslims" (a group that included a small minority of adherents *across* all of the four racial groups considered in this study) faced discrimination. If a respondent believed that his or her own group faced as much discrimination as "Muslims," or more, that respondent, I suggest, was expressing perceptions of in-group anxiety, or "embattlement."

Less than 1 percent of the U.S. population identifies as "Muslim," and Muslims are at least twice as likely to report being the victim of religiously motivated hate crimes as members of any Christian religious group in the country.[24] Still, it is important to note that while

Table 3.4 *Perceptions of In-group Embattlement Among Evangelicals and Non-evangelicals, by Race, 2016*

	Whites Face as Much Discrimination as Muslims, or More	Muslims Face More Discrimination Than Whites
White (n = 1,035)	37%	63%
White and born-again (n = 191)	49	51

	Blacks Face as Much Discrimination as Muslims, or More	Muslims Face More Discrimination Than Blacks
Black (n = 3,102)	84%	16%
Black and born-again (n = 1,062)	86	14

	Latinx Face as Much Discrimination as Muslims, or More	Muslims Face More Discrimination Than Latinx
Latinx (n = 3,003)	62%	38%
Latinx and born-again (n = 577)	63	37

	Asian Americans Face as Much Discrimination as Muslims, or More	Muslims Face More Discrimination Than Asian Americans
Asian American (n = 3,006)	40%	60%
Asian American and born-again (n = 486)	45	55

Source: Author's calculations based on 2016 CMPS.
Note: Data are weighted.

about 66 percent of Americans as a whole believe that Muslims face more discrimination than Christians, this sentiment is reversed among white evangelicals. In a 2013 Public Religion Research Institute survey, nearly 60 percent of all white evangelicals claimed that Christians face more discrimination than Muslims. This sense of embattlement can be extended beyond religious in-groups.

For the analysis presented in table 3.4, I created the same measure of perceived in-group embattlement for each of the four racial groups, with "Muslim" used as a proxy for the out-group. Again, these categories are not mutually exclusive. (A member of any racial group could identify as "Muslim" and vice versa.) However, since Muslims constitute a minority of all of the aggregate racial groups considered here, "Muslims" serves as a very rough proxy for a potential out-group. The in-group is the respondent's own self-identified racial group. My question is, to what extent is a sense of perceived in-group embattlement associated with political attitudes?

The results are clear. The analysis in table 3.5 shows cross-tabulations across racial groups and policy attitudes that distinguish (1) those who believe that their group faces as much discrimination as Muslims, or more, from (2) those who believe that Muslims face more discrimination than their group. From table 3.4, we know that the proportion of the former is greater among white evangelicals (49 percent) compared to whites who are not evangelical (37 percent). The analysis in table 3.5 includes "born-again" identifiers only. For the white evangelical sample, believing that whites face the same level of discrimination as Muslims or more is associated powerfully with taking the most conservative position on every political issue examined, from voting for Trump in 2016 to opposing government intervention on climate change to taxing the rich. All of those associations are statistically significant ($p < .05$). For Latinx and black evangelicals, perceived in-group embattlement is not associated with taking any conservative position. The political attitudes of those who believe that their group faces the same amount of discrimination as Muslims or more are not very different from the attitudes of those who believe that Muslims face more discrimination. Among Asian Americans, perceived in-group embattlement is lower than among whites, and less consistently associated with conservative attitudes on policies. However, in their beliefs about immigrants hurting the economy, climate change, disagreement that the U.S. government should apologize for slavery, and opposition to the Black Lives Matter movement, Asian American evangelicals who exhibit a sense of in-group embattlement are more conservative than those who do not.

Multivariate analysis (not shown) isolates the effects of in-group embattlement among the white evangelical sample from a host of other variables, including socioeconomic status, party identification, generalized conservatism, age, and economic anxiety. Further analysis also shows that these results are not a function of region (such as living in the South). In other words, in-group embattlement is not a proxy for any of these other measures, but a distinct explanation for the policy attitudes observed here.

Table 3.5 *Perceptions of In-group Embattlement and Political Attitudes Among Evangelicals, by Race, 2016*

	Believes Whites Face as Much Discrimination as "Muslims," or More	Believes "Muslims" Face More Discrimination Than Whites	Believes Blacks Face As Much Discrimination as "Muslims," or More	Believes "Muslims" Face More Discrimination Than Blacks	Believes Latinx Face as Much Discrimination as "Muslims," or More	Believes "Muslims" Face More Discrimination Than Latinx	Believes Asian Americans Face As Much Discrimination as "Muslims," or More	Believes "Muslims" Face More Discrimination Than Asian Americans
Agrees that a ban on same-sex marriage is needed	57%*	41%*	37%	37%	41%	43%	39%	35%
Voted for Trump in 2016 (registered voters only)	89*	59*	7	5	29	33	41	33
Republican Party identification	77*	61*	8	11	23	32	35	30
Agrees that immigrants hurt the economy	66*	34*	22	20	26	21	29*	15*
Disagrees that the federal government should combat climate change	39*	16*	9	7	11	9	15*	3*

Disagrees with increasing taxes on the wealthy	40*	18*	6	8	12	17	15	8
Disagrees with providing more federal funding to aid the poor	29*	12*	4	3	9	8	15	11
Disagrees that the United States should apologize for slavery	79*	45*	13	16	25	35	36*	18*
Opposes Black Lives Matter movement	77*	29*	6	14	17	25	27*	13*

Source: Author's calculations based on 2016 CMPS.

Notes: Data are weighted. These results obtained in further multivariate analyses (not shown) controlling for partisanship, socioeconomic status, attendance at religious services or gatherings, socioeconomic anxiety, southern residence, and general conservatism (the belief that the federal government almost "never" does the right thing). Same sizes: black, n = 1,062; black Trump voter item, n = 744; Latinx, n = 577; Latinx Trump voter item, n = 355; Asian American, n = 486; Asian American Trump voter item, n = 191; white, n = 244; white Trump voter item, n = 136.

*p < .05

Contexts and Connections

Of course, a sense of in-group embattlement does not develop in a vacuum and is not the only explanation for why nonwhite evangelicals exhibit much more moderate political viewpoints than white evangelicals. Socioeconomic circumstances also seem to be a small part of the explanation, but with the exception of attitudes about same-sex marriage, white evangelicals still appeared to be more conservative across the board than black, Latinx, and Asian American evangelicals when income and education were held constant. In addition, black, Latinx, and Asian American evangelicals exhibited very different levels of average income and education, yet each of these groups was much more moderate than the white evangelical group. The survey data used throughout this book has an important limitation: failing to capture fully the social contexts that shape religious communities. But we do know from both the 2016 CMPS results and our site visits that these contexts vary tremendously, largely because religious spaces remain racially segregated. This variability in social contexts probably matters for political attitude formation because it affects information flow and the sharing of norms. For example, as Paul Djupe and Christopher Gilbert contend, differences in political attitudes should be expected even within the same religious tradition as a result of variation in both broad social settings and the local, often church-based social networks through which political information flows.[25]

Djupe and Gilbert would argue that broad racial differences in political attitudes among evangelicals may be established in local, racially specific social contexts, as "individuals may come to their political decisions not just through religious influence, but because of their involvement with others in a religious setting."[26] Because the social networks in evangelical churches tend to be racially homogenous, the content of political discussion in evangelical communities will reflect social interactions shaped by racial context.[27] Although these interactions vary across local congregations and degree of involvement in small groups and other religiously based social structures, a trickle-up effect is probably reflected in the systematic effects observed in the current study.[28]

Brian McKenzie and Stella Rouse provide a related explanation having to do with the theological emphasis in white versus nonwhite religious settings.[29] They argue that because places of religious worship remain racially segregated, the spiritual development of these communities is likely to take place in different cultural settings or contexts. A strong majority of evangelicals claim that they attend a racially homogenous place of worship. The racial context, then, remains quite distinct for both white and nonwhite evangelicals. McKenzie and Rouse suggest that nonwhite communities place more emphasis on social justice, norms of community, and minority social location. They further contend that "White religious assemblies differ slightly because they primarily serve Whites, who are the majority population. . . . In these settings, minority group status and issues of marginality are not regular topics of theological reflection."[30] Variations in the political attitudes of different religious communities along racial lines may in part be explained by differences in theological interpretation and emphasis in white and nonwhite religious settings.

Although social networks are not the focus of this study, they may help to explain the results. For example, as Robert Putnam and David Campbell observe, interreligious ties weaken intolerance.[31] It is plausible that a greater potential for interreligious ties among Asian Americans and Latinx tempers their political agendas as well. We might attribute differences in political attitudes between white and Latinx and Asian American evangelicals to the fact that evangelical Christians make up a smaller number and proportion of both the Latinx and Asian American populations compared with the white population. Sixty percent of Latinx identify as Catholic, and Catholicism has been a dominant cultural force among Latinx in the United States. Most Latinx are likely to have some close friends and family members who do not consider themselves evangelical or born-again Christians. Similarly, the Asian American community is religiously diverse and includes a large proportion (about 20 percent) of people who describe themselves as religiously unaffiliated. Again, we would expect Asian Americans to have friends and interact with relatives who do not identify as born-again or evangelical. Further, Latinx and Asian Americans tend to have more racially diverse discussion networks than whites.[32] Future studies might investigate the degree to which interreligious ties and interracial interactions vary across racial categories and the effect of these ties on political attitudes across groups.

Conclusion

Spirituality was critically important to the black, white, Latinx, and Asian American evangelicals interviewed for this project. Most respondents relied on the Bible for spiritual guidance, found their Christian communities to be a source of everyday support, and prioritized their relationship with God and Jesus. Despite these shared characteristics, the voices featured in this chapter suggest that racial identity and experience as members of racial minority groups tempers the political attitudes of evangelical Latinx and Asian Americans compared to those of their white counterparts. I argue that though they share similar theological beliefs and practices, white and nonwhite evangelicals have different conceptions of national community and that this may well account for why Asian American and Latinx evangelicals are more progressive with regard to public policy than white evangelicals.[33] Nonwhite evangelicals are more likely to adopt a sense of national community that extends beyond their fellow religious adherents, and this broader perspective in turn creates a different political orientation from that of their white evangelical counterparts. In addition, differences in political attitudes across race in white versus nonwhite evangelical churches may be attributed to the tighter association in white churches between religious identity and partisanship and to the distinct political cues that occur in these different evangelical churches. Finally, the findings in this chapter point to a sense of in-group embattlement as a powerful driver of conservative political attitudes among white evangelicals and, to a lesser but still notable extent, Asian American evangelicals.

CHAPTER FOUR

IMMIGRATION TRENDS AND EVANGELICAL COMMUNITIES

The two previous chapters established that there is a great deal of variation among evangelicals in their political attitudes. White evangelicals, as a group, are more conservative politically than black, Latinx, or Asian American evangelicals. This study shows that race is such a powerful part of American politics that, with the exception of attitudes toward abortion and same-sex marriage, black, Latinx, and Asian American evangelicals are much less conservative than even whites who do *not* identify as evangelical. In addition, when we examine each racial group separately, it appears that white evangelical attitudes, compared to those of nonwhite evangelicals, are more powerfully motivated by a sense of in-group embattlement—the belief that one's own group faces as much discrimination as an out-group, like Muslim Americans, or more.

At the same time, it would be premature to suggest that progressive elements in the United States have a lock on the political loyalties of nonwhite evangelicals. Latinx and Asian American evangelicals in particular exhibit more conservative attitudes than their non-evangelical coethnics. Politically, these groups are in the moderate middle, they are growing fast, and they may be the only source of future growth in the evangelical voting bloc. Here we take a closer look at how Latinx and Asian American evangelicals, who are fueling demographic change in the evangelical community, come to adopt an evangelical identity and how their experiences both connect them with and distinguish them from the majority-white evangelical community.

Coming to a Born-Again and Evangelical Identity

Latinx and Asian Americans come to their evangelical identity through conversion or through living in an evangelical household. According to the Pew Research Center, in 2013, while only 14 percent of Latinx were raised Protestant, 22 percent reported their current religious affiliation as Protestant.[1] In contrast, there were more Latinx who left their childhood religion of Catholicism than there were Latinx who are currently Catholic. In the same report, about 40 percent of all Latinx who were currently Protestant reported that they were raised Protestant. The vast majority of Latinx Protestants consider themselves born-again.[2] Religious switching among Latinx is very slightly more prevalent among the U.S.-born than the foreign-born. Further, about the same proportion of foreign-born Latinx switched faiths prior to migration as those who did so after migration to the United States.[3]

Among Asian Americans, conversion to Protestantism is also a driver of evangelical faith. While about 17 percent of Asian Americans surveyed by Pew in 2012 claimed to have been raised Protestant, 22 percent of those surveyed claimed to be Protestant currently.[4] Approximately 40 percent of U.S.-born Asian Americans have switched religions, versus 30 percent of foreign-born Asian Americans. The Pew data on Asian Americans do not include questions about their pre- or post-migration conversion.

Stories of conversion were quite common among those interviewed for this project. For instance, a Filipina woman who was born in the United States in 1976 grew up in a Roman Catholic household and attended Catholic elementary, middle, and high school. She became a born-again Christian during her freshman year in college, when her roommate shared the gospel and invited her to attend her church.

In a Spanish-language interview, a first-generation Mexican American immigrant woman in her forties described her conversion experience. She said that she grew up in a Catholic household but had converted to Christianity four years prior to the interview:

> What's the difference between the Catholic religion and the Christian religion? Well, just the fact that—at least for me, since I grew [up] in a Catholic environment—I never understand what it meant to be a Catholic. I got to see the difference when I started attending a

Christian church. I know that I can talk directly to God, right? And I don't have to get on my knees or [ask] favors to a statue or something like that—to an image. I speak directly to God, and God will answer according to our faith.

How was I introduced to Christianity? Okay, it's going to be four years in January, and it happened because of a conversation that I had with a friend—the one who invited me there. I was going through a very difficult ordeal—I had a family situation—and she invited me to go to her church. She invited me to go there, and my first interview was with the pastor of the church. I talked to him about the situation that I was going through. They prayed for me, and ever since they prayed for me I felt that peace and that healing on my body and my soul. That made me want to keep going there, and I also realized that I could talk to God the same way I am talking to you right now—and that would give peace to my soul.

Others were raised in evangelical households. For instance, a thirty-year-old Korean American man from Irvine, California, "grew up in a Christian family. Church was an everyday Sunday activity, from the get-go. So ever since I was a child all the way until high school, Sundays were church days." Similarly, a Mexican American woman, born and raised in Texas, attended a Baptist church with her family growing up and continued in that tradition as an adult. She noted, "I guess I've always—I grew up in a church. My mother and father attended church, so we went to church all the time. That's my background there."

The warm and welcoming environment of evangelical churches was palpable in many of the places of worship I visited, and it stood in especially stark contrast to the anti-immigrant rhetoric that has characterized the public sphere of late. Many immigrant Asian Americans and Latinx described the inclusive, familial atmosphere. For example, many Latinx evangelical churches adopt an explicitly open attitude toward immigrants. A Mexican American immigrant woman from Zacatecas, Mexico, said that her evangelical church was quite welcoming to immigrants:

They come in and say, "I have no place to live, I don't have a home, I come from Durango," or whatever state they're from. There are many who arrive from different places saying they have no place to live, I have no food, and so I know that in the house of God, God is going to help me. . . . And so we know that a lot of people come, just like us, coming from a far place where someone can steal from you along the way, where suddenly they may get lost and they have nothing to get by, and so we help them in whatever we can and later on they slowly settle in.

Church members often support one another on a day-to-day basis as well. For example, a young Korean American mother who attended an evangelical Presbyterian church described how church members helped a fellow member whose child was ill:

I mean, I see it. Actually, one of the kids was actually kind of sick at the beginning, so they prayed for them and a lot of people came by and brought them food, to do whatever they could do. So everybody has rallied around them and thank God, everything's okay now, but it was a bit of a crisis for the first two months.

A second-generation Chinese American woman who attended a Southern Baptist church in Anaheim, California, also discussed the close connection between church members:

We have a lot of young couples in our church, and some of them have been fortunate enough to have twins or quadruplets. The church members have been great about lending a hand in terms of cooking meals and babysitting and helping with a lot of those things, for example. Or if there's someone in the hospital, they [the church members] will visit and pray with others.

A retired Mexican American man from Texas who identified as Pentecostal explained that in times of need, his church members would help each other "in whatever needs that arise in their situations, whether it be physical or spiritual."

Marco Witt, pastor of the Spanish-language service at Lakewood Church in Houston, described his personal connection with many of the members of his megachurch. Each week he held a welcome line and greeted any of the members who wished to have a personal moment with him after the service.

Humanity. Humanity is hurting. Humanity has got needs. Humanity is anxious. We live in anxious times. You don't have to read the newspaper headlines to realize people are anxious. My line takes forever because we're all hugging each other and we're kissing each other and we're crying with each other and kissing all the babies.

These examples show that for many adherents the church is not only a place of spiritual practice but also an important source of social support. Given this function, it is perhaps not surprising that Asian Americans and Latinx, particularly the foreign-born, are joining evangelical churches in relatively large numbers.

Day-to-Day Life as an Evangelical in Asian and Latinx Communities

Evangelical Christians tend to score high on traditional measures of religiosity, such as daily prayer and church attendance. For instance, a 2015 Pew-sponsored study observed that "one in eight adults in America are regularly attending an evangelical church, but fewer than one in 25 Americans show up to a mainline church nearly every week."[5] Political scientists note a high correlation between religiosity and support for the Republican Party. Most important for the study of evangelicalism and political attitudes, however, is attention to the ways in which, as Lydia Bean makes clear, spiritual and religious life take place not only at the site of worship but in every aspect of many evangelicals' lives, including at the voting booth.[6] Many of those interviewed for this study fostered their connection with God and their religious community beyond attendance at a Sunday service. Describing the importance of his spiritual identity, a Latinx Pentecostal man who attended a multiracial church in southern California said, "It's not just going to church and going to church on Sundays and then after that you do whatever you want to do, it's not that. It's twenty-four hours, seven days a week, just walking with the Lord with love and trust and hope and helping others. It involves the whole community. It's not just yourself, but you're helping your family, your neighbors, and all people around."

A Japanese American man who attended a Holiness church in West Los Angeles also described his religious commitment beyond the Sunday service:

> It's the core of my identity. I mean, the goal in my life is not religion per se, but my relationship with Christ would be preeminent. That is my goal. That's what I strive for. Specifically how that plays out every day, I try to make it a point to meditate on scripture every morning, to read a piece of the Bible a little bit in the morning, to pray throughout the

day, keeping in dialogue with God throughout the day, not just with difficult tasks, try to keep a dialogue with God going every day, and hoping that through that relationship, as I meditate on God's word, as I pray, that that would begin to affect my desires, the way I think, my behavior, and my attitude towards people.

Similarly, for Mariana, an evangelical woman from El Salvador in her late forties, being a "follower of Christ" was an essential part of her day-to-day life. Mariana was born into a Catholic family in El Salvador; after her mother died, her father eventually remarried a Protestant woman. In her teens, Mariana had a conversion experience when she attended church with a friend. Since that time, she said, "in every decision, I always pray and ask for the guidance of God in all things."

Although a high level of religious devotion was not a criterion for being interviewed, many evangelicals expressed their Christianity as a lived experience that anchored every part of their lives. For example, a thirty-eight-year-old Mexican American man interviewed in Spanish was asked about what drew him to his current place of worship and how his spirituality manifested itself in his sense of community and identity.

> I think that this is where God brought me, to this church. It was God who brought me to this church. . . . It's my relation with Jesus Christ, okay. I am in the process, like all Christians should, of deepening that, making that relationship more intimate. As I repeat, it's not a religion, it is a relationship, and also integrating the principles that Jesus Christ left us for use in our daily lives, in all aspects: in making decisions, guiding people, not judging others, etc.

This interviewee took part in many church activities outside of the Sunday service, through various ministries. He was part of a ministry for men, a program that offered opportunities for spiritual growth, provided service activities, and encouraged social connections among the men in his church. He was also part of a marriage ministry, which helped couples navigate marriage through moral and spiritual guidance. In addition, he participated in a hospital ministry that relied on volunteers like him to visit members of the church who had been hospitalized.

To give a final example of the ways in which interviewees characterized their spiritual lives, Elliot, a Korean American man who attended a nondenominational church in Santa Monica, California, described religion as playing a "large role" in his life: "Not just in morals and ethics, but in every aspect of how I live, I check back to what the Bible would say in my response to certain situations or how I would ethically or morally conduct myself. So basically it would be foundational for anything I would do. I try my best." Over the years, Elliot had taken on more responsibilities at his church. He was deacon of the education ministry, leading the Sunday service for children in the church. He was also a youth group leader. He led a small group meeting for college students during the week. In addition, he was part of a small group meeting during the week with some men in their thirties and forties, and he also participated in a Bible study group.

These examples illustrate some of the ways in which Asian Americans and Latinx experience religion as a major aspect of their lives that informs their everyday outlook and their relationships with others. They also illuminate the more moderate political attitudes exhibited by Asian American and Latinx evangelicals, which are more likely a function of racial identity, community boundaries, and a racialized context than of differences in religiosity or religious beliefs.

Connections to Broader Evangelical Communities

The dispersed and independent nature of evangelical churches is well established. The sociologist Christian Smith describes the evangelical church culture as "decentralized" and "fragmented."[7] More recently, Lydia Bean and Steven Teles claim that the failure of church elites to move evangelicals on a progressive climate change agenda is evidence of the loose organizational structure that characterizes the national community of evangelical churches in the United States.[8] In many cases, they suggest, national evangelical leaders are not on the radar screens of local churchgoers because there is no recognized leadership hierarchy. One of their key informants supported this claim:

> That's the curse of the evangelicals: we don't have one hierarchy. There's probably 100,000 gatekeepers, and 100,000 gates. Every local pastor in some way is a gatekeeper, and on independent Baptist churches, where each congregation really stands alone. Nobody has kind of the ecclesiastical authority to say, "I speak for everyone." If any of you do that, you hear, "The hell you do. You don't speak for me."[9]

Bean's research emphasizes the critical role of lay leaders, rather than pastors or official church leadership, in communicating political cues to their fellow members.[10] At the same time, the evangelicals interviewed for this project did access Christian radio, books, and other religious materials. Very occasionally, Asian American and Latinx evangelicals would report reading or listening to nationally recognized evangelical leaders, such as the progressive evangelical pastor Rick Warren or James Dobson, founder of the conservative evangelical Focus on the Family organization.

Elliot, the Korean American evangelical man described earlier, said that he frequently consulted Christian books and listened to Christian radio, "just because it helps in my spiritual growth, in my spiritual walk. That's not to say that that's all I read, listen to, or watch on TV. I listen to sports radio just as much as Christian radio. In a perfect world, all you'd listen to would be Christian things that would aid your spiritual growth. However, we're all human, we have other interests as well." He stated that he gravitated toward Christian materials to bring himself "closer to God." Another interviewee, a Chinese American woman who attended an evangelical Covenant church in Irvine, California, also read Christian books and listened to Christian radio. She said that when she was dating, she would read spiritual guides to relationships. For her professional life, she relied on Christian books about leadership. She listened to radio shows produced by Family Life (a network of Christian radio stations) and podcasts produced by the conservative Christian organization Focus on the Family.

Interviewees rarely suggested that they consulted Christian materials or resources to better understand political issues, but one Chinese American Southern Baptist woman from Anaheim, California, did say that she consulted "different Christian websites" for information and opinions about political issues.

The Christian materials that we collected from evangelical places of worship for this project—which included bulletins, newsletters, and pamphlets—did not directly engage policies, political parties, or candidates. Rather, they emphasized local resources and spiritual guidance, and they underscored a sense of community among Christians. In this respect, they contributed to the positioning of Asian American and Latinx evangelicals within a local and national Christian community, but did not strongly or consistently connect them to the white evangelical mainstream.[11]

Evangelicals in "Ethnic" Churches

The membership of evangelical churches is becoming more racially diverse, but the overall picture is one of racial segregation. This segregation may help to explain why we see real differences in political attitudes and in the sources of those attitudes across racial groups. The vast majority of individual places of worship in the United States are dominated by a single racial group—that is, at least 80 percent of the attendees share the same racial background. Mark Chaves and Alison Eagle note that while far more white evangelicals are now part of a congregation with at least "some" nonwhite members than was the case in the past, it remains true that fewer than half of white congregations could be described as including any recent immigrants.[12]

Most, though not all, of those who participated in an in-depth interview for this study belonged to a church with a congregation made up primarily of people of the same racial background. This is not surprising given the trends described here. Moreover, the racial homogeneity of these places of worship was noted by both pastors and laypeople. In one poignant conversation, an Asian American pastor who led a small church in Houston described his efforts to create a multiracial church. His congregation was predominantly Asian American, and they occupied a space that had been recently used by a predominantly black congregation whose pastor had left their church. The Asian American pastor invited all of the previous occupants to remain as part of the new church, and some did. Over time, however, fewer and fewer non–Asian Americans attended the church. He speculated that it was partly the visual impact of entering a church with a mostly Asian congregation that made non–Asian Americans uncomfortable.

A pastor of a Latinx church in Houston discussed the racial divide in American evangelical churches as in part a language divide:

> I think in the religious community, and I'll go out on a limb here, 'cause this is, like, completely unscientific, but it's my gut feeling, my gut feeling is that a lot of Hispanic community doesn't even know what's going on in the English evangelical community, don't have a clue. Because in the U.S., they don't have to worship in the English circles. There's Spanish Christian churches all over this country, and the growth of those churches is unbelievable.

Several Asian Americans explained why they attended pan–Asian American churches. A Korean American woman who attended a large Evangelical Covenant church in Irvine, California, said of her church:

I think it is ethnically somewhat diverse. Most churches are polarized along ethnic lines, significantly, but we're predominantly an Asian American church, so there are a lot of different Asian subgroups. Chinese and Korean tend to be the two most dominant ethnic groups. The last time we did a census, I believe it was somewhere around 20 to 25 percent Chinese and the same for Korean, and it was somewhere around 15 percent Japanese, and around 8 to 10 percent Caucasian, and then everybody else falling into the remaining—somewhere in that range.

The racial makeup of the church was one of the things that drew her to attend it. She observed, "You go to other churches that have a similar feel, similar music, similar sermon, but it's predominantly Caucasian, it's white America, and you don't necessarily feel like you fit in totally or you're a novelty sometimes." She explained that her husband was white, but had grown up in Hawaii, a predominantly Asian American state. Because he had experienced being a member of a racial minority group in Hawaii, she said, he also felt comfortable in a pan–Asian American church.

Political Communication in Latinx and Asian American Evangelical Churches

Conservative churches are sometimes assumed to be environments of heavy-handed political socialization, with pastors leading their flocks not only spiritually but also politically. This view was perhaps given some support in 2014, when 1,600 pastors openly defied a federal law prohibiting tax-exempt religious organizations from endorsing political candidates.[13] The Alliance Defending Freedom organized the pastors, claiming that the federal law "unconstitutionally restricts free speech."[14] As of 2016, more than two thousand pastors had violated the law, according to the Alliance Defending Freedom website.[15] However, only a small number of potential violations were investigated by the Internal Revenue Service.

Pastors are allowed to discuss political issues so long as they maintain the prohibition against candidate endorsement. However, when asked about the extent to which they had heard overtly political messages from their pastors, very few of those interviewed for this project claimed to have heard any such messages. And in more than sixty site visits to churches in Los Angeles and Houston between 2006 and 2008, my project team never heard a pastor endorse a candidate. In fact, political messages were far from the norm. The most common theme of any sermon in an ethnic church was one's personal relationship with Jesus. A Filipino American man described his pastor's sermons as follows:

> My pastor, a lot of his messages or his sermons, he tries to really focus a lot of them on day-to-day issues that we just as humans go through every day. So a lot of what he preaches is geared towards, how do you interact with coworkers? How do you interact with people who have done things to you that you couldn't forgive? So, issues of forgiveness and things like that. It's a big part, because at the same time, he gears them towards those issues that we're gonna be facing every day. But I know a lot of the messages aren't necessarily geared toward society in general.

Another interviewee said that his pastor did discuss political issues and candidates from a partisan perspective. He said of his pastor, "I know that he's a Republican and he likes to vote completely for the party. Sometimes he says, 'Let's vote for this particular issue.' Some people don't like it when he says that, and they're right." Note this interviewee's pushback against the pastor's attempt to influence his membership's political views. It was very common for interviewees to know their pastor's view on politics, but also to express their own, often differing, opinions. For example, when asked about whether her pastor expressed political views, a Mexican immigrant woman in Houston who attended the Spanish-language service of a megachurch said, "He does not tell us to do certain things because he feels this or that or because he is with the Republicans or Democrats. Simply to vote and it is important to vote. Also to hold in our prayers for whomever we are going to vote. Yeah, he has never said, 'Vote for this person.'" A Filipina American woman who attended a Bible-based evangelical church in Los Angeles described her pastors' ideas about politics: "I think through their values I have an idea. . . . They really encourage us to select our leaders that share our same morals and cultural values." She added, with a laugh, "I'm assuming that they voted for [the Republican candidate]." Nevertheless, even though both of her pastors were very much "pro-life," she noted, "they don't tell us who to vote for."

A Korean American man in his midthirties who attended a nondenominational evangelical church in Santa Monica said that one of his pastors did not disclose his political affiliation, but he did encourage voting. Another pastor at his church was "a little more vocal," but he still limited his political expression even on issues such as abortion, "because he feels that the more Christians scream bloody murder regarding that, it's not going to change any hearts and minds in people." When asked how he had come to understand the political views of his pastors, he claimed that he learned of their views mainly through "discussion groups," but also "oftentimes in sermons, and just professionally."

Most interviewees agreed that political information was conveyed informally rather than through sermons. For example, during a question-and-answer session of a small-group Bible study, church members might ask informal questions of their pastor, "because the pastor is relaying the word of God to you," said an Asian American man in his thirties who attended West Los Angeles Holiness Church. "Ultimately, like I said, every issue that he covers we would have to always go back to the Bible. If the Bible supports a certain issue, then the pastor will probably view it in that way also. Once again, the pastor and the Bible go hand in hand." The informal nature of political communication was emphasized again and again in interviews. Describing his pastor, one member of a panethnic Asian American evangelical church in Sugarland, Texas, said, "Pastor Joe is careful not to say anything politically in the pulpit. First of all, you can be taxed as an entity by Uncle Sam." Yet he also regularly talked to his pastor about politics in informal settings, noting that his pastor was "very political in the sense—in his private life, where we can talk."

Political discussions tended to revolve around traditional issues taken up by religious conservatives. For example, the Korean American man who attended a nondenominational church in Santa Monica claimed that, in his church, "I guess homosexuality is the base issue, not that we focus on that, just because it's a blatant issue that for us we have a clear view on and it seems like it just gets accepted more and more in the secular world, in real life. When I think of any one social issue, that comes to mind." At the same time, he noted that "politics doesn't end up being a focal point of our conversation at church, because that pretty much tends to take you away from God and you start to think about just worldly things. In our church, we try not to be worldly, but to focus on God. That would be the primary focus of the church." This political environment is quite different from the stereotypical image of the evangelical church as a hotbed of political talk and political socialization.

As noted earlier, pastors at ethnic churches do raise issues of race. For example, at Jorge's church, his Filipino American pastor would not only take a hard stance against abortion and same-sex marriage but also discuss racism in society: "He himself is Filipino American. He's shared a lot of his personal experiences on racial issues. I guess it kind of aligns with what I believe as well. He knows that there's people in the world that have racist attitudes. . . . He's still willing to serve them or to reach out to them, even though he knows that they have a certain ideology."

And in some of their churches, according to the interviewees, politics was simply never a topic addressed, even informally. For instance, Josefina claimed that she had never heard other members talk about politics. Neither did her pastor. "I have never heard him speak about politics, never. Never from the pulpit. And I have never spoken to anybody in the church about politics. I mean, they might be involved themselves, I don't know." Josefina expressed some reservations about the church taking a strong role in political affairs. She was skeptical of those who "don't think with their heart, they think with their religion. If they would think with their heart, then they would know how to go about it, but they get so fanatical, they really just destroy what Christianity really is." Josefina made a distinction between her religious beliefs and her political choices: "I'm against abortion, but I'm not going to keep from voting for a president just because he is for abortion. I'm not a fanatic about things. I'll look at things with my heart, not my head or my religion."

In her study, Bean maintains that "churches avoided 'political' talk, understood as explicit persuasion or deliberation about political subjects."[16] Instead, political distinctions and positions are shared through informal small-group interactions and one-on-one conversations that do not center on clear partisan divides but rather provide cues about the boundaries of the national Christian community and the duties that accompany Christian identity. In the United States, religious identity can be linked to more conservative political positions precisely because politics is not an *explicit* part of the religious experience. Rather, it is very subtly but consistently embedded in everyday interactions in members' spiritual lives.[17] In this way, politics is "in the air," but it is not an explicit topic of sermons or interpersonal dialogue in many evangelical churches. It is plausible that the politics "in the air" of ethnic evangelical churches is different from what circulates in predominantly white evangelical places of worship.

How Will Asian American and Latinx Evangelicals Fit into American Politics in the Future?

Because they are emerging groups in American politics, the political attitudes and behavior of Latinx and Asian American evangelicals are not well established. Assessments of the partisan attachments of Latinx and Asian Americans rely heavily on assumptions related to race *or* religion.

Their racial identities and associated issues are largely seen as driving Latinx and Asian Americans as a whole toward the Democrats.[18] Meanwhile, issues related to religious identity are sometimes seen as a distinct advantage for the Republicans. For example, some pundits suggest that increasing numbers of evangelical Latinx may create a new constituency for Republicans. Commenting in *Time* magazine after the 2012 presidential election, the journalist Elizabeth Dias speculated that Latinx evangelicals might "help Republicans take a bite out of the Democratic advantage with Hispanic voters" because "they prize the nuclear family. They are largely against abortion and gay marriage. They also tend to be wealthier than Latino Catholics."[19] This comment echoes Pastor Mario Bramnick, who told a National Public Radio reporter in 2016, "For most Latinos, not only Hispanic evangelicals, family values are important, social values are important."[20] These perspectives are consistent with earlier speculation that increasing numbers of Latinx evangelicals would contribute to the political power of conservative Christians.[21]

In contrast to wide speculation about the political leanings of evangelical Latinx, there has been little commentary on Asian American evangelicals and their political orientations. Still, there is some conjecture about Asian American voters more generally. For example, even in the face of overwhelming support for President Obama among Asian American voters in 2012 (nearly 70 percent), some pundits claimed that the group's "natural home" was the Republican Party: "Everyday observation of Asians around the world reveal them to be conspicuously entrepreneurial, industrious, family-oriented, and self-reliant. If you're looking for a natural Republican constituency, Asians should define 'natural.'"[22]

In fact, Asian Americans have been leaning away from Republicans in recent years. Since the mid-1990s, they have demonstrated the strongest shift toward the Democratic Party of any racial group in the United States.[23] These trends have not been divorced from discussions about religion in American politics. Scholars of Asian American politics attribute the Asian American shift toward the Democrats over the past twenty years in part to the Republican Party's association with conservative Christians. The political scientist Karthick Ramakrishnan, for instance, explains that Asian Americans' Democratic leanings may be related to the GOP's pro-Christian image: "a party projecting a pro-Christian image makes it difficult to reach out to Asian American voters, most who are not Christian."[24] Most Asian Americans are not Christians. But at 42 percent, Christians represent a significant plurality of Asian Americans.[25] Evangelical Christianity is growing among Asian Americans over time, but it is unclear if their support for the Republican Party will increase as a result.

A case study of immigration reform helps us begin to think about one of the primary questions raised in this book: To what extent are growing numbers of Asian American and Latinx evangelicals converging with or diverging from the traditional white evangelical voting bloc? Despite their growing numbers, Latinx and Asian evangelicals do not seem to be moving their white counterparts on the issue of immigration.

Immigration as a Case Study of Racial Divides in Evangelical America

In the national debate over immigrant rights, one of the most visible evangelical leaders on the national front is the Reverend Samuel Rodriguez, president of the National Hispanic Christian Leadership Conference. Rodriguez is based in Sacramento, California. In the spring of 2006, he spearheaded an effort within the evangelical community to encourage political leaders to support comprehensive immigration reform, with an emphasis on creating a pathway to legalization for the country's estimated 11 million undocumented immigrants. More than fifty evangelical leaders endorsed a letter to President George W. Bush and Congress calling for policies to create a path to legal residence for undocumented persons already living in the United States and provide humane border protection.[26] Rodriguez often underscores Latinx evangelicals' growing numbers in both the electorate and in the evangelical community.[27] In 2016, he claimed that his organization serves nearly 15 million Latinx born-again Christians in 40,000 congregations in the United States.[28]

In May 2007, Reverend Rodriguez joined with other evangelical leaders, including the Reverend Jim Wallis, founder of the liberal-leaning Christian organization Sojourners, to form the national organization Christians for Comprehensive Immigration Reform (CCIR). That group conducted a media outreach and letter-writing campaign to mobilize congregants in evangelical churches in presidential-election swing states to support comprehensive immigration reform. It also organized prayer vigils for comprehensive immigration reform in more than one hundred places across the nation during President Obama's second month in office.[29] In April 2009, the CCIR released a public statement praising Obama for his promise to hold discussions on immigration reform within his first year of office.

Even with the "new prominence" of leaders like Rodriguez in the public debate over immigration, some evangelical leaders have been reluctant to join the coalition seeking comprehensive immigration reform.[30] In fact, the largest, most established evangelical Christian organizations, including the Christian Coalition, the Family Research Council, and the National Association of Evangelicals, did not endorse the 2006 letter or join the CCIR.[31] These leaders may have been taking a cue from the white evangelical rank and file. Surveys conducted over the past fifteen years suggest that white evangelicals harbor more conservative views on immigration than other religious groups, or Americans in general. A 2006 study from the Pew Research Center showed that 63 percent of white evangelicals believed that "the growing number of newcomers from other countries threatens traditional American customs and values," compared to 48 percent of all Americans and

51 percent of white mainline Protestants.[32] Similarly, 64 percent of white evangelicals surveyed in 2006 believed that "immigrants today are a burden because they take our jobs, housing and health care," compared to 52 percent of all Americans and the same proportion of white mainline Protestants.[33]

Even in the midst of a national campaign by Rodriguez and other evangelical leaders to build support for immigration reform among the rank and file, white evangelicals have been the religious group most opposed to a path to citizenship for unauthorized immigrants.[34] In fact, while support for a path to citizenship for undocumented immigrants had slowly been ticking up among rank-and-file white evangelicals from 2009 to 2013, in 2014 support dipped more among this group than any other religious group.[35] This trend was identified in a unique study by the Public Religion Research Institute and the Brookings Institution. Those organizations interviewed a representative sample of people in 2013 about their immigration views and reinterviewed the same people in 2014. The dip was unexpected, because the hard-won support for comprehensive immigration reform and a path to citizenship remained strong among some prominent evangelical elites.[36]

In 2016, in the months leading up to the presidential election, white evangelicals appeared to have moved even further to the right on immigration issues. In that year, 63 percent of white evangelicals described immigrants as "a burden" on the United States, compared to 43 percent of Americans overall.[37] While a majority of Americans (61 percent) favored a path to citizenship for "immigrants living in the U.S. illegally," just 49 percent of white evangelicals favored a path to citizenship for this group.[38]

Rodriguez has been outspoken in his disappointment with white evangelical leaders who refuse to join the coalition and has expressed his dissatisfaction with them on multiple occasions:

> My message to the white evangelicals would be [that] Hispanic immigrants resonate more with your values than many other constituencies or groups. They are God-fearing, hard-working, family-loving people. And if that doesn't look a lot like the Joneses and Smiths of Alabama and Arkansas and Michigan, other than the color of their skin, I don't know what would.[39]

In June 2015, Donald Trump, in announcing his intention to run for president of the United States, rallied the crowd with what many perceived as anti-immigrant and anti-Latinx rhetoric when he discussed U.S. immigration policy: "When Mexico sends its people, they're not sending their best. . . . They're sending people that have lots of problems, and they're bringing those problems with us. They're bringing drugs. They're bringing crime. They're rapists. And some, I assume, are good people."[40] Rodriguez, who gave the benediction at the 2012 Republican National Convention, shot back at Trump:

> To date Donald Trump's comments about immigration have been inflammatory, impractical and unhelpful. Now that he is the presumptive nominee, we call upon him to immediately stop rhetorical commentary he has previously used that discredits groups, including Latino immigrants, and start discussing and offering real, productive solutions for comprehensive immigration reform.[41]

Rodriguez is not the only Latinx evangelical leader to gain national prominence by encouraging U.S. lawmakers to create a path to citizenship for undocumented immigrants. Gabriel Salguero, president of the National Latino Evangelical Coalition (NaLEC), has also been at the forefront of these efforts. Salguero led a multiracial congregation in New York City, the Lamb's Church of the Nazarene, for much of his career; then, in 2015, he accepted a job as a pastor at Iglesia El Calvario, a megachurch in Orlando, Florida. In March 2010, Salguero published an article on the popular progressive Christian website Sojourners to explain why he was joining a national march for immigrant rights in D.C. that month:

> Simply stated, as a Christian I am mandated to love my neighbor as myself without prejudice to origin, color, or creed. Jesus himself reminds Christians to "welcome the stranger" in Matthew 25. In addition, the Torah of the Hebrew Scriptures reminds us continually to be kind and merciful to the stranger, widow, and orphan. In the end a nation is judged by how it treats the most vulnerable among them. My faith compels me to speak with the immigrants and their families.[42]

In 2012, Salguero gave the benediction at the Democratic National Convention.

For this book, I interviewed a megachurch pastor, Marco Witt, who leads the Spanish-language service at Lakewood Church in Houston. Witt described his efforts to convince white evangelical leaders to move to the left on immigration reform—efforts that have met with very limited success:

> I will go on record as saying this. To me, it's been unfortunate to see the white evangelical community completely miss the point on immigration. They missed it completely. It doesn't have to do with breaking the law or not. There is a moral law. There's a greater humanity law at stake here. And that's the second part that I'll unpack for you, because the whole law part, then, those of us who came down on the side of helping the immigrant, then all of a sudden we were looked at as these lawless, flaunting our nose, flipping our noses at the law. No. See, what the greater community forgot to point out is, yes, these immigrants crossed the border. A law was broken. You know what kind of law it is? It's called a federal misdemeanor. It's the same kind of law that's broken when anyone gets a traffic ticket. It's in the exact same category.

Witt went on to discuss the tension felt by some leaders pushing for comprehensive immigration reform in 2006. He said that he was an early supporter of a policy that would create a path to citizenship for undocumented immigrants and that his position was not well received by some white colleagues. Although Joel Osteen, the English-language pastor at Witt's church in Houston, signed on to comprehensive immigration reform, many of Osteen's "big name [white evangelical] friends" would not follow suit. Witt lamented that he "couldn't get any of them to issue a statement in favor of immigration reform. Not a single one of them. Not a single evangelical leader. It was one of the most discouraging things that I have gone through. I was able to get three people." He noted that some did not care about the issue, and some were vehemently opposed. Witt's frustration reflects a major divide in the evangelical faith community, one underscored by my interviews with rank-and-file evangelicals.[43]

A View from the Pews

Every Spanish-language interviewee in this study mentioned immigration as a critical issue discussed among their fellow religious adherents, and all supported a path to citizenship for undocumented immigrants in the United States. This is perhaps to be expected, as Latinx, evangelical and otherwise, are more supportive of immigration reform than other groups.[44] A thirty-seven-year-old Spanish-speaking evangelical man who attended Marco Witt's Spanish-language service in Houston claimed that immigration was often discussed among his fellow religious adherents, along with social security, welfare, scholarships, and similar issues. Witt had asked members of the church to pray for immigration reform and to write letters to Congress.

Support for a path to citizenship among Latinx evangelicals interviewed in English and among Asian American evangelicals was more mixed. For instance, a Chinese American woman in her late thirties who attended a Southern Baptist church in Anaheim took a relatively hard-line position when it came to immigration reform:

> I am for stricter border control. However, I do find that there's a point where there does need to be a streamlining in the immigration process so that people can get here legally and they don't have to jump the lines. It's all about incentive. And of course you can't just round up, like, three million people and send them all home. There's logistical issues with that. But as far as arguing the principle, I believe we need stricter borders. Stricter enforcement of immigration policy.

Similarly, some English-speaking Latinx interviewees also expressed conservative views on the issue of immigration. For example, a woman who attended a Baptist church in Houston claimed that she held different views on immigration than many who attended her Sunday Bible study group. "I have talked to some people about immigration. They have different views than I do because some are for immigration, and I'm not. . . . I mean, I don't have anything against immigration. I do have very strong reservations against illegal immigration." Her opposition to unauthorized immigration was religious to some extent:

> I know I hold very, very strong views against illegal immigration. Sometimes I'm thinking, "Okay, am I thinking with my heart or am I thinking with my head?" 'Cause there's these people that are wanting to come to the U.S. to better their life. But also, I think about how this country was founded, and it was under God, and the laws are there for

us to uphold. And the illegals have come over here illegally and think that they have a right to stay here just because they want a piece of the dream that they call it. But to me, that's not right. If they want to come to the U.S., they need to do it legally, not illegally. But what I'm seeing, and all these people that are crying for amnesty, they think that they have a right to be here.

Others interviewed for this project expressed deep concern for the plight and future of unauthorized immigrants. A Mexican American man who attended an Assemblies of God church in southern California said that he viewed policies through a Latinx lens at times: "Not because I have a problem, because thank God I'm a citizen now and I have a job and I'm okay, but there's other people, other Latinos, friends, they are struggling with that. They need for immigration to have better policies for them, for those who have been here for the longest time, to become—if not citizens, to become legal here."

A Puerto Rican immigrant discussed his sympathy with other Latinx who were unable to obtain citizenship and faced deportation.

I feel sometimes it's unfair the way the Anglos, the way they feel like— you know, the way we have to limit the immigration, change laws or whatever. I feel like sometimes the people that have been here for so many years, and now they're saying they have to send them back to their countries, I feel like they should have a limit to all of this, that there's been people living here in the States after maybe ten or fifteen years, they should make a way possible that they could easily become citizens, not make it so difficult for them. I don't know if it's that they can't drive, make it hard for them to get a license unless they're citizens.

A Korean American woman who attended a Korean evangelical church in Irvine noted that while her Christian identity was all-encompassing, because of her Asian American identity, she also identified with other nonwhite immigrants and their issues: "I definitely see Korean Americans as minorities. So some of the issues that Mexican immigrants go through, or Vietnamese immigrants, they all seem the same to me."

These sentiments stand in sharp contrast to the views expressed by the white evangelicals interviewed for this project.

White Evangelicals Push Back on Immigration Reforms

Conservative views on immigration were the norm among the white evangelicals interviewed for this project, though their attitudes were complex. For example, a white evangelical man from Santa Clarita who described himself as "Baptist-Pentecostal-evangelical" explained his beliefs about immigration policy in the United States:

> I think immigration is a good thing, legally. That's the bottom line. I think that the illegal problem is a big deal. . . . I know that there's families that want to better themselves, and I have friends, people I know, that are probably illegal. I've gotten to know them. I talk to them about God and so forth. I care for them as people. . . . What I'm against is our government spending money to basically hand out stuff to people that are here illegally, [here] illegals can get health care or credit cards. An illegal alien can get a credit card from Bank of America. They can get health benefits and all this other kind of stuff that Americans can't even get.

The Affordable Care Act ("Obamacare") and most state health care programs bar undocumented immigrants from receiving health care benefits. Still, interviewees expressed concerns about extending health care benefits to those in the country without documents. Another white evangelical, Paula, who attended an Assemblies of God church in California's Simi Valley, associated immigration with growing diversity in the region:

> I am now becoming very aware of the immigration problem. And more and more aware of—and I can't say it's fear, but it's a recognition and disapproval of Mexico attempting to take over California, well, actually, the U.S. . . . It'll take many years, but our whole community is being taken over. The Mexicans are trying to become dominant in our area. The black people are trying to become dominant in Los Angeles. And I'm definitely beginning to feel like a minority myself.

Paula also expressed concerns over "the Islamic attempt to take over the world" and noted that she was "sad and mad that we as Christians were asleep for many years and are just really waking up to the need to stand up and be counted as Christians." Paula linked immigration to her own anxieties about the decline of Christian America. She buttressed her remarks with a reminder that "our nation was truly founded by Christian men on the word of God."

Robert Jones notes that the real growth among evangelicals is going to be among Latinx: "The very same people that are causing changes to happen in their [white evangelical] community are the people they're looking to bring in religiously."[45] Jones's observation highlights a dynamic that is absolutely critical to understand. Demographic transformation does not necessarily lead to political transformation. In fact, even as historically white churches see their numbers shrinking, they may react to demographic change more defensively than receptively. At the same time, as I have shown, there is not uniform support for a path to citizenship among Latinx and Asian American evangelicals. And because they hold more conservative views than their non-evangelical coethnics, it would be a mistake to assume that Latinx and Asian American evangelicals will simply add their numbers to the Democratic Party and progressive coalitions.

Other religious issues may even complicate efforts around immigration reform. A bill introduced in Congress by former Representative Mike Honda (D-CA) in 2013 provides a prominent example of how Latinx and Asian American evangelicals' support for comprehensive immigration reform may be compromised by other religious priorities. Honda's Reuniting Families Act sought to expand family-based immigration visas and included provisions enabling gays and lesbians to sponsor a same-sex partner.[46] The Reverend Samuel Rodriguez reacted strongly to the bill, claiming that it was an affront to his efforts. He told a reporter on the Christian Broadcasting Network that the inclusion of the same-sex partner provisions in the bill would "dilute, will fracture [the comprehensive immigration reform] coalition that includes the Hispanic Evangelical Association, Southern Baptists, other major denominations that have signed on to Comprehensive Immigration Reform. We will all pull out."[47]

Rodriguez's reaction echoed his response to a similar bill that Honda introduced in 2009. At that time, he claimed that the expansion of immigrant family sponsorship categories to same-sex partners was offensive to his efforts and "a slap in the face of those of us who have fought for years for immigration reform."[48] Further, he indicated that any attempt to include language that would advance the status of gay and lesbian partners through immigration law would split the coalition: "Good luck trying to pass comprehensive immigration reform without the faith community behind you."[49] Honda's 2013 bill died in the House Judiciary Committee, but Rodriguez's remarks underscore the potential tensions between traditional immigrant rights advocates and "new players" such as evangelical Christian leaders.

Rodriguez has long emphasized the unique perspective that he believes Latinx evangelicals bring to the debate over immigration and other pressing issues in the United States: "In the culture wars, Hispanics are on the values side. But social justice is more a part of our ethos [than for other evangelicals]. We're attuned to poverty, homelessness, AIDS. We have a more complete vision of the gospel."[50] By June 2016, however, despite his apparent alignment with the progressive agenda on immigration, Rodriguez seemed to have moved toward the Republican presidential nominee, Donald Trump, a candidate he had earlier criticized for expounding harsh anti-immigrant rhetoric. As the 2016 campaign season progressed over the summer, Rodriguez appeared to support the Republican candidate, claiming that he "resonated" with Donald Trump on "religious liberty, on the sanctity of life, on addressing Christian persecution around the world, but not only around the world, but here in America."[51] Further, Tony Suarez, the executive vice president of Rodriguez's National Hispanic Christian Leadership Conference, was recruited to serve on Trump's "Evangelical Executive Advisory Board."[52]

Gabriel Salguero, the head of the National Latino Evangelical Coalition, may have led prayers at Democratic National Conventions, but he has long cautioned that the Latinx evangelical vote is up for grabs. He wrote in a 2016 New York Times op-ed that "Latino evangelicals are invested in a holistic view of justice that includes decreasing poverty and expanding the pro-life movement to include the abolition of the death penalty. This makes evangelical Latinx the ultimate swing-voting block: Slim majorities supported both George W. Bush and Barack Obama."[53] Salguero holds a conservative stance on abortion, but his organization was also the first national evangelical group to oppose the death penalty.[54] Thus, Salguero's stance on "life" issues is not easily characterized as Democratic or Republican, but in his view, it is internally consistent: "All life is precious. . . . We're pro-life: womb to the tomb."[55]

Conclusion

This chapter has provided a brief overview of day-to-day life among Latinx and Asian American evangelicals, particularly in terms of politics. Focusing on the issue of immigration to highlight racial splits in the evangelical community, we have seen that white evangelicals tend to take a conservative position on this issue, particularly when it comes to undocumented immigrants, while Latinx and Asian American evangelicals are more open or moderate.

These political rifts may be expected when it comes to immigration. After all, Asian Americans and Latinx are more likely to be foreign-born than their white counterparts. But as I have emphasized in this book, this political divide is not limited to immigration but extends across a range of political issues. What matters here is that these political divides may not play out in predictable ways. Meanwhile, however, the agenda of white evangelicals, who have resisted change in the face of Asian American and Latinx newcomers, has prevailed in recent times.

CHAPTER FIVE

CONCLUSION: THE PERSISTENCE OF THE RIGHT IN AN ERA OF DEMOGRAPHIC CHANGE

Race matters in shaping evangelical political attitudes, and this book has shown that there are major differences in the politics of white versus nonwhite born-again Christians. Simply put, white evangelicals are much more conservative politically, across a broader range of political issues, than black, Latinx, or Asian American evangelicals. This is true even after we take into account important influences such as party identification, economic resources, and economic anxiety. This book has also established that conservative political attitudes, particularly those outside of the traditional evangelical agenda, can be traced to the distinct ways in which many white evangelicals conceptualize the boundaries of their national community and their perceived in-group embattlement in the face of demographic change. That perceived in-group embattlement remains an important driver of a conservative political agenda, uniquely distinct from party identification, socioeconomic status, general conservatism, and economic anxiety and region (the South).

When I began this project, I was fascinated by the growing numbers of Latinx and Asian American evangelicals, who, at least at first glance, appeared to be a potential new force in American politics. However, the 2016 presidential election and the critical role of white evangelicals in Donald Trump's victory provided a powerful reminder that demography is not destiny in American politics.[1] In the aggregate, white evangelicals appear to be supporting a political agenda that goes against the tide of demographic change in the United States.

The Advantages of the White Evangelical Voting Bloc: Structures of Empowerment, Ideology, Identity, and Organization

The white evangelical voting bloc is buttressed by several structures that reinforce its advantages, enabling it to resist the challenges to its strength posed by demographic changes. These structures have to do with geographic settlement patterns and political mobilization. At the same time, nonwhite evangelicals confront many of the same barriers to political empowerment faced by progressive white evangelicals in terms of relatively low numbers in the population and weaker ideological and identity formations.

Geographic and Political Structures Trump Demographic Change

Despite the attention to demographic change in the United States, political change does not always track population change. Although the Asian American and Latinx populations have undoubtedly grown, racial categories are not stable, nor are population changes linked to racial transformation. Pew Research Center researchers D'Vera Cohn and Andrea Caumont claimed in 2016 that, "by 2055, the U.S. will not have a single racial or ethnic majority. Much of this change has been (and will be) driven by immigration. Nearly 59 million immigrants have arrived in the U.S. in the past 50 years, mostly from Latin America and Asia."[2] Nevertheless, the political impact of this anticipated demographic transformation is unclear.[3] Aside from debates about whether projections of demographic change exaggerate the decline of those who identify as white, long-standing structural conditions ensure that white Americans will be overrepresented in terms of political power for some time.[4]

First, whites are overrepresented in the electorate compared to their proportion of the population.[5] In the 2016 presidential election, exit polls estimated that 71 percent of voters were non-Hispanic white, but the U.S. Census Bureau shows that they made up only 61 percent of the total U.S. population that year.[6] Also, as Nate Cohn has noted, national exit polls may *underestimate* the proportion of the electorate that is non-Hispanic white.[7] Many observers have noted that Latinx and

Asian American voters are the fastest-growing segments of the electorate, but that they remain underrepresented among voters compared
to their population numbers owing to lower eligibility rates (lack of
citizenship, lack of registration, and proportion of the population
under age eighteen) and lower rates of turnout, even among the eligible.[8] The demographer William Frey illustrated the population-voter
gap well, even in 2004:

> For Hispanics in particular, their growing population does not trans-
> late directly into voters. Because they are younger than the general
> population, one third of Hispanics are below voting age, and more
> than a quarter are not citizens.
>
> For every 100 Hispanics in the population, only 40 are eligible to
> vote, 23 are likely to register, and just 18 will show up at the ballot box.
> The voter-to-population translation is almost as low for Asians, where
> only 21 out of 100 people will likely vote. For blacks the number is 37,
> and for whites, almost half.[9]

These gaps remained in 2017.[10] White evangelicals are also disproportionately represented among voters, making up about 21 percent of the total
U.S. population but 26 percent of all voters in 2016.[11]

Second, both whites and white evangelicals have a disproportionate
population advantage in competitive swing states and in the Electoral
College. Overall, whites are more likely to reside in battleground states
than nonwhites.[12] Take Florida, sometimes called "the swingiest swing
state in the nation" owing to its bounty of twenty-nine Electoral College
votes and its historic role in determining presidential fates.[13] According
to the Center for Economic and Policy Research, "White people tend
to live in states where their vote counts more, and minorities in places
where it counts less. This means that the Electoral College not only can
produce results that conflict with a majority vote, but it is biased in a
way that amplifies the votes of white people and reduces the voice of
minorities."[14] White evangelicals are disproportionately concentrated
in the South, the Republican geographic stronghold in the United States
for the past fifty years. They also account for the largest religious groups
in the swing states of North Carolina, Virginia, and Ohio.[15]

Third, research suggests that whites, particularly those who live in
battleground election states, are more likely to be mobilized politically
than other groups.[16] Data from the 2016 CMPS show that among white

and Latinx citizens who identified as born-again, about 25 percent of each group affirmed that they had been "asked to register or to vote by a candidate for office or a person working for a candidate, a representative of a political party, or someone from an organization working in [their] community" (within the past twelve months). However, these data also show that only 16 percent of Asian American citizens who identified as born-again were contacted about registering or voting.

Though these geographic and structural realities will certainly change over time, they remain important to understanding why demographic change will not ensure immediate political change within evangelical communities.

Progressive White Evangelicals: Identity and Ideology

The challenges that face politically progressive white evangelicals vis-à-vis their conservative white evangelical counterparts must also be taken into account when assessing the current political power of Latinx, Asian American, and black evangelicals.[17] In particular, politically progressive white evangelicals have faced limits on their political power not only because they are less numerous than conservative white evangelicals but also for reasons based on ideology, identity, and group cohesion.

For instance, progressive evangelicals lack a political agenda that aligns fully with the political priorities of either of the two major parties. In an article that describes politically progressive evangelicals as "outsiders on the inside," Brandon Withrow suggests that progressive evangelicals adopt a political agenda that is not easily recognized as part of partisan orthodoxy.[18] Withrow points to the newly formed group Public Faith as an example of a progressive evangelical organization that could challenge the traditional Christian Right. Public Faith is "composed of both conservative and liberal leaning Christians. They oppose climate change, racial injustice, and poverty, but remain traditional on issues of abortion and gay marriage."[19] This "mixed" political agenda is not unlike that of the Latinx and Asian American evangelicals discussed in this book. While the two major parties may see these ideologically moderate groups as the ultimate swing voters, thus far they seem much more comfortable mobilizing "a sure thing," that is, their traditional ideological and demographic bases; this strategy leaves progressive and nonwhite evangelicals somewhat ignored.[20]

The historian and religious scholar Alec Ryrie attributes the political "weakness of the [evangelical white] religious left" to a failure to assert a meaningful religious identity in the public sphere.[21] Progressive white evangelical leaders such as Brian McLaren, a white evangelical pastor whose popular writings seek to challenge the view that "conservative Republican" and "evangelical Christian" go hand in hand, and Jim Wallis, founder of the progressive evangelical organization Sojourners, have risen in prominence. Progressive evangelicals have not been able, however, to grow their political presence at the mass level, Ryrie contends, because they have been unable to advance their religious identity when asserting political views. In their commitments to tolerance and openness, progressive white evangelicals, according to Ryrie, are reluctant to organize around Christianity for fear that they will alienate minority religious groups, such as Muslims and Jews. His contention is that in their deep adherence to a multifaith, multicultural United States, it is "very hard for those on the left to unapologetically put their faith at the heart of their politics."[22]

In other words, though progressive white evangelicals cannot be accused of perpetuating hegemonic Christianity, they may find it difficult to mobilize as progressive Christians when their participation in politics does not put their religious identity front and center. Ryrie argues that progressive white evangelicals are most limited by their own competing commitments to faith *and* an inclusive religious culture, rather than by "secular bullies" on the political left. Tellingly, Ryrie notes that among black, Latinx, and Asian American evangelicals, churches are less likely to be seen as religious institutions than as ethnic institutions. Hence, asserting Christian faith may also prove to be a barrier to political empowerment among both progressive white evangelicals and nonwhite evangelicals. Here it is interesting to note that religiosity may even be negatively related to civic engagement among Latinx in general.[23]

Finally, Withrow argues that progressive white evangelicals face challenges to political empowerment because they lack organizational coordination. Progressive evangelical organizations exist, he claims, but "tend to remain siloed."[24] Latinx evangelical organizations such as the National Hispanic Christian Leadership Conference and the National Latino Evangelical Coalition have facilitated political coalition-building among Latinx who identify as born-again Christians, but there is little coordination or centralized leadership among Latinx evangelical churches. There is even less among Asian American evangelicals and across nonwhite evangelical churches more broadly.

In addition to the structural and geographic disadvantages that are likely to limit the political power of nonwhite evangelicals in the near future, they may also, like progressive white evangelicals, see their political power challenged by (1) their moderate and ideologically disparate political agendas; (2) an inability to successfully advance a religious identity within progressive circles; and (3) weak organizational cohesion among religious leaders and institutions.

Revisiting the Boundaries of Community and In-group Embattlement

An emerging literature traces the long and intimate relationship in U.S. politics between religious identity and racial identity.[25] Nancy Wadsworth contends, for example, that "wherever race appears in American political history, religion is never far away."[26] One of the theoretical assumptions flowing from this observation is that the foundational categories of race and religion in the United States have been constructed in relation to one another.[27] Racial categories give religious categories meaning and vice versa, such that "the denominational and sociological configurations of American religion developed through racial divisions."[28] Along these same lines, Andrew Greeley and Michel Hout suggest that both black and white evangelicals identify with a "single powerful religious story" and devote their political loyalties to "the party that best reflects the collective self-image" informed by their story.[29] This book attempts to move beyond the black-white comparison to better understand how religious identity works to influence the politics of growing numbers of Latinx and Asian Americans in the United States, but it also raises up the potential importance of white identity and community formation within evangelical America.

Important for this project is the argument by scholars of race and religion in American politics that, similar to the intersection of gender, race, and class categories, race and religion operate together and simultaneously to influence individual political positions and outlooks.[30] For those familiar with the literature on intersectionality, applying an "intersectional identities" framework to the categories of race and religion may raise some questions because these theories are concerned with multiple axes of *marginalization*.[31] Also, while many non-Western religious identities are certainly marginalized in the U.S. context, others, like Protestant Christian identities, are often considered dominant in U.S. society. Further, in many, though not all, cases, religious identity is considered more of a matter of personal choice than identities such as race and gender.[32] For these reasons, this book does not apply an intersectional identities framework to the case of race and religion. However, it does take seriously the theoretical claim that multiple identities associated with race and religion may be mutually constitutive and work in tandem to influence an individual's political orientations.

To understand how race and religion work together to shape political attitudes, this book focuses on distinct conceptions of community boundaries and perceptions of in-group embattlement among different groups of evangelicals. Theoretically, the interdisciplinary concept of boundary-making is critical here. Social theorists have long attended to boundary-making as a fundamental process of social interaction. As Michèle Lamont and Virág Molnár point out in their excellent essay on "The Study of Boundaries in the Social Sciences," the concept of social boundaries drives Durkheim's treatment of the "sacred" versus the "profane," Marx's claims about the conflict between different economic classes, and Weber's analysis of status groups, particularly ethnic groups.[33] Most important for the research presented in the current study is the notion of "symbolic boundaries." Cynthia Fuchs Epstein argues that while boundaries may be "mechanical and physical," they may also "be conceptual and symbolic."[34] Symbolic boundaries, according to Epstein, vary in meaning, but this variability does not detract from their social power. Rather, because individuals may attach their own meanings to symbolic boundaries, boundaries are maintained even in the face of different interpretations.

In this book, I argue that white and nonwhite evangelicals' very different conceptualizations of the boundaries of their communities may lead to their distinct policy attitudes. As Lydia Bean also argues, white evangelicals in the United States may be less likely than their nonwhite counterparts to view marginalized groups, such as "the poor," "immigrants," and people of color, as belonging within the boundaries of their community.[35] Past research suggests that white evangelicals are more likely to prefer same-race neighbors than are Catholic, Jewish, or non-religiously affiliated whites.[36] This is what we would expect given my hypotheses about the boundaries of community among white and non-white evangelicals. I am not suggesting that white or nonwhite evangelicals have made explicit efforts to develop or maintain particular boundary conceptions. As Epstein points out, symbolic boundaries may be the product of "the unnoticed habits and language of every-day life vigilantly attended to by family and friends, business associates and colleagues, or in individual or collective guilt derived from shared values."[37] Susan Fiske goes perhaps even further, arguing that boundary-making and the perceptions of in-groups and out-groups are both ubiquitous and automatic.[38]

Boundaries separate people and groups, a function that "invariably results in inequality."[39] In her study of gender and the workplace, Epstein shows that boundaries between men and women are maintained as a result of perceived threats over material and social territory, but also over identity and sense of self, worth, authority, and hierarchy.[40] Scholars have engaged in empirical studies of the nature of boundaries and variations in tolerance and exclusion.[41] I build on this work here, hypothesizing that differences in how white and nonwhite evangelicals define "us" and "them" are at the heart of their policy differences. White evangelicals, I suggest, are more likely to define "us" as prototypical members of their own group (white evangelicals) than are nonwhite evangelicals.[42] For many, support for conservative policies reflects their interest in maintaining resources for their own group. But that is not the only dynamic that seems to flow from the different conceptions of community boundaries held by white and nonwhite evangelicals.

Stemming from dominant perceptions among white evangelicals about community boundaries and "who we are" may be feelings of anxiety and a sense of peril about external threats to those boundaries and the identities they maintain. I show in this book that part of what underlies white evangelicals' more conservative policy attitudes compared with the attitudes of nonwhites is the belief that whites face as much discrimination as outgroups, such as Muslims, or even more. About half of white evangelicals in this study held this belief, and those who hold it are likely to support conservative policy positions across a range of issue areas. This measure, I believe, captures a sense of white embattlement against a changing world. Others have noted this phenomenon as well. For example, the ethnographer Marla Kefalas, in a study of a working-class white neighborhood in Chicago, observed that "what Beltway-dwellers seek to protect is not so much racial homogeneity as a shared vision for their community."[43] On average, white evangelicals were more likely to feel that whites faced discrimination than were non-evangelical whites. It is not difficult to extrapolate from the findings presented here that those most likely to express a sense that whites are embattled also fear the loss of a "shared vision for their community." They perceive that their way of life is imperiled. As I noted in chapter 3, Christopher Parker and Matt Barreto as well as Algernon Austin forward similar arguments in their treatments of two other (mostly white) politically conservative groups—Tea Party supporters and "Obama-Haters."[44]

Religion matters in U.S. politics, but in many important respects, it interacts with racial identity and racialized geographies, racial boundary-making, and feelings of peril.

What Does the Future Hold for Evangelicals and Politics?

Demographic change will bring political change in evangelical America, but the political transformation will not be straightforward.[45] Yes, "whites are becoming a smaller share of America's evangelical world."[46] Today whites make up less than two-thirds of all evangelicals, and only 50 percent of all evangelicals under age thirty are white.[47] Even within the next eight years, white Christians, as a whole, will face a demographic challenge when it comes to political power: "By the 2024 presidential election," Robert Jones notes, "even if the GOP could secure every single white Christian vote, these votes would land 3 points short of a national majority."[48]

Demographic change within the evangelical community will not translate into immediate political change, but population shifts will eventually change the direction of evangelical politics. I predict that, against the backdrop of a steady or declining white evangelical population, the political impact of growing numbers of Asian American and Latinx evangelicals, though not sweeping, will be felt most acutely in areas of stark partisanship (support for Republicans on the presidential ticket) and in areas related to broad government programs and interventions, such as government-sponsored health care, taxation of the wealthiest Americans, and climate protection.[49] These policy areas are characterized by dramatic differences of opinion between white and nonwhite evangelicals.

Second, much of what is predicted here will depend on issue salience and political mobilization. Latinx and Asian American evangelicals remain staunch opponents of abortion for the most part.[50] Despite the strong association of the Democratic Party with abortion rights, evangelical Latinx and Asian Americans have continued to support Democrats at higher rates than they have supported Republicans. It may be that abortion has not been a salient political issue in recent elections. Because the political mobilization of Latinx and, especially, Asian Americans remains relatively low compared to whites and blacks, the potential effects of political mobilization on the politics of evangelical Latinx and Asian Americans are unclear. In part because of the GOP's calculated political strategy and mobilization, white evangelicals have come to view support for the Republican Party and its platform as a critical expression of *religious* identity and conviction. The party has not directed its energies at Latinx and Asian American evangelicals in the same way, but the Republicans are more likely to make such a move than the Democrats, who rarely appeal to religious identity and have thus far failed to mount a mass-mobilization campaign targeting either Latinx or Asian Americans more generally.

At the same time, it is important to recognize that there is a significant amount of variation among nonwhite evangelicals. Black evangelicals exhibit more progressive attitudes on almost every policy issue, including immigration, than Latinx or Asian American evangelicals. In a dynamic similar to white evangelicals, Asian American evangelicals show some sense of perceived in-group embattlement in a limited set of issue areas, particularly issues related to racial justice for blacks and immigrant rights. Nonwhite evangelicals are far from homogeneous politically, though they do appear markedly more progressive overall than their white counterparts. In addition, there are important cleavages within the broad panethnic categories of "Asian American" and "Latinx." One of the most important cleavages in these two populations is immigrant generation.[51] The scholarship on political attitudes among Asian American second-generation immigrants suggests that the children of immigrants are more progressive than their first-generation parents on a range of political issues.[52] The literature on Latinx first- and second-generation immigrant political attitudes is more mixed. Some researchers have found, for instance, that native-born Latinx are more conservative toward undocumented immigrants than their foreign-born counterparts.[53] These patterns portend change, but uneven change.

Evangelicals as a Case Study of U.S. Politics

In 2013, South Carolina senator Lindsey Graham warned his fellow Republicans that they were entering "a demographic death spiral"—an implicit reference to the political consequences of decades of Asian and Latinx immigration.[54] In the lead-up to the 2016 presidential election, a *Washington Post* headline predicted that population change in the United States, specifically immigration from Asia and Latin America, would result in nothing less than "the coming Republican demographic disaster."[55] The conventional wisdom about demographic change and the fortunes of the Republican Party came under serious question, however, with the victory of Republican Donald Trump in 2016, after he ran on a promise to get tough on immigration.

In this book, I argue that there are major political distinctions between whites and nonwhites who share the same religious identification. And yet the political opinions of Asian American, Latinx, and black evangelicals have not influenced the overall evangelical policy agenda in a dramatic way. The reasons why conservative white evangelicals dominate the policy agenda of "evangelicals" more generally, and the tenacity of this group in the wider sphere of American politics, are partly revealed here. The populations of Asian American and Latinx evangelicals may be growing, but growth in their political power—limited by their geographic concentration, ideological profile, lower levels of political participation, and organizational capacity and coordination—has not been commensurate. In this respect, the experiences of Asian American and Latinx evangelicals mirror those of Asian Americans and Latinx in the broader U.S. political arena and provide a glimpse into the evolution of U.S. politics—though it will surely take place, change going forward will be slow and marked by uneven political victories and representation.

APPENDIX: 2016 COLLABORATIVE MULTIRACIAL POST-ELECTION SURVEY

Methodology

A total of 10,145 completed interviews were collected online in a respondent self-administered format from December 3, 2016, to February 15, 2017. Both the survey and the invitation were available to respondents in English, Spanish, simplified Chinese, traditional Chinese, Korean, and Vietnamese. Because of the primary interest in the 2016 election, the project started with a large sample of registered voters to provide large sample sizes for analyses. The data also include an adult sample of nonregistered voters, including noncitizens.

The full data are weighted within each racial group to match the adult population in the 2015 American Community Survey one-year data file for age, gender, education, nativity, ancestry, and voter registration status. A post-stratification raking algorithm was used to balance each category within plus or minus 1 percent of the ACS estimates.

The survey's main focus is on attitudes about the 2016 election and candidates, debates over immigration, policing, and racial equality, and experiences with racial discrimination across many facets of American life.

The median interview completion time was 43.2 minutes.

Data for registered voters come from the national voter registration database email sample, and respondents were randomly selected to participate in the study; they confirmed that they were registered to vote before starting the survey. For the nonregistered sample, email addresses were randomly selected from various online panel vendors.

In total, 298,159 email addresses were selected and sent invitations to participate in the survey, and 29,489 people accepted the invitation and started the survey, for an effective response rate of 9.9 percent. Among the 29,489 people who started the survey, 11,868 potential respondents were terminated because quotas were full, which resulted in 17,621 who were eligible to take the survey. Of these, 10,145 completed the full questionnaire, for a cooperation rate of 57.6 percent.

Respondents were given a $10 or $20 gift card as compensation for their participation.

Nonregistered voters were randomly selected from one of six online panels of respondents from Federated, Poder, Research Now, Netquest, SSI, and Prodege, and they confirmed that they were not registered to vote before starting the survey. Programming and data collection for the full project were overseen by Pacific Market Research in Renton, Washington.

In keeping with best practices and data transparency ethics in the social sciences, the original survey data will be posted to Inter-university Consortium for Political and Social Research (ICPSR) after four years, which is expected to be early 2021.

Table A1.1 *Characteristics of Self-Identified Evangelical or Born-Again Christians in Houston and Los Angeles Who Participated in Qualitative Interviews, 2007–2011*

Interview Number	Gender Identity	Race-Ethnicity	Age	Location	Language of Interview
1	Female	Asian American (Taiwanese)	50	Houston suburb	English
2	Female	Asian American (Singaporean)	48	Houston suburb	English
3	Male	Asian American (Chinese)	60	Houston suburb	English
4	Male	Asian American (Indian)	n/a	Houston	English
5	Male	White	64	Houston suburb	English
6	Female	Asian American (Korean)	51	Southern California	Korean
7	Female	Asian American (Korean)	54	Southern California	Korean
8	Female	Asian American (Korean)	49	Southern California	Korean
9	Male	Asian American (Korean)	51	Southern California	Korean
10	Female	Asian American (Korean)	30	Southern California	English
11	Male	Asian American (Korean)	30	Southern California	English
12	Female	Asian American (Korean)	38	Southern California	English
13	Female	Asian American (Korean)	37	Southern California	English
14	Male	Asian American (Filipino)	30	Southern California	English
15	Female	Asian American (Korean)	35	Southern California	English
16	Male	Asian American (Chinese)	41	Southern California	English
17	Male	Asian American (Japanese)	29	Southern California	English
18	Female	Asian American (Chinese)	33	Southern California	English
19	Female	Asian American (Chinese)	36	Southern California	English

(continued)

Table A1.1 (*continued*)

Interview Number	Gender Identity	Race-Ethnicity	Age	Location	Language of Interview
20	Male	Asian American (Korean)	30	Southern California	English
21	Female	Asian American (Filipino)	32	Southern California	English
22	Female	Asian American (Taiwanese)	32	Houston suburb	English
23	Female	Latinx	n/a	Houston	English
24	Female	Latinx (Mexican)	37	Houston suburb	English
25	Female	Latinx (Mexican)	n/a	Houston	English
26	Female	Latinx (Colombian)	54	Houston	English
27	Male	Latinx	n/a	Houston	English
28	Male	Latinx (Colombian)	51	Houston	English
29	Male	Latinx (Mexican)	45	Houston	English
30	Male	Latinx	n/a	Houston	Spanish
31	Female	Latinx (Salvadoran)	40	Houston	Spanish
32	Male	Latinx	38	Houston	Spanish
33	Male	Latinx (Colombian)	45	Southern California	English
34	Male	Latinx (Mexican)	82	Southern California	English
35	Male	Latinx (Puerto Rican)	61	Southern California	English
36	Male	Latinx (Mexican)	60	Southern California	English
37	Female	Latinx (Mexican)	51	Southern California	English
38	Female	Latinx (Puerto Rican)	60	Southern California	English

39	Male	Latinx (Mexican)	Southern California	English
40	Female	Latinx (Mexican)	Southern California	English
41	Male	Latinx (Mexican)	Southern California	English
42	Female	Latinx (Salvadoran)	Southern California	English
43	Male	Latinx (Puerto Rican)	Southern California	English
44	Male	Latinx (Colombian)	Southern California	Spanish
45	Female	Latinx (Mexican)	Southern California	Spanish
46	Female	Latinx (Mexican)	Southern California	Spanish
47	Male	Latinx (Nicaraguan)	Southern California	Spanish
48	Female	Latinx (Salvadoran)	Southern California	Spanish
49	Female	Latinx (Guatemalan)	Southern California	Spanish
50	Female	Latinx (Mexican)	Houston	Spanish
51	Male	Latinx (Peruvian)	Houston	Spanish
52	Female	Latinx (Mexican)	Houston	Spanish
53	Female	Latinx	Houston	Spanish
54	Male	Latinx	Houston	Spanish
55	Male	White	Southern California	English
56	Male	White	Houston	English
57	Male	White	Southern California	English
58	Male	White	Southern California	English
59	Female	White	Southern California	English
60	Female	White	Southern California	English
61	Female	White	Southern California	English
62	Male	White	Southern California	English

(continued)

Table A1.1 (*continued*)

Interview Number	Gender Identity	Race-Ethnicity	Age	Location	Language of Interview
63	Male	White	41	Southern California	English
64	Male	White	53	Southern California	English
65	Male	White	33	Southern California	English
66	Male	White	28	Southern California	English
67	Female	White	28	Southern California	English
68	Male	Black	21	Southern California	English
69	Male	Black	20	Southern California	English
70	Female	White	33	Houston suburb	English
71	Male	Black	32	Southern California	English
72	Female	Black	24	Southern California	English
73	Male	Black	52	Southern California	English

Source: Author's compilation based on original interview data, 2007–2011.
Note: n/a = not available.

Table A2.1 Policy Positions of Evangelicals, by Race, 2012

	Voted for Obama (Democrat) Versus Romney (Republican) in 2012 Presidential Election		Favors Government-Sponsored Health Care (2010 Affordable Care Act)		Favors Raising Taxes on the Wealthy to Provide a Middle-Class Tax Cut	
	Evangelicals	Non-evangelicals	Evangelicals	Non-evangelicals	Evangelicals	Non-evangelicals
White	26%	60%	13%	44%	51%	62%
Black	85	95	70	62	75	71
Latinx	69	76	50	53	64	68
Asian American	54	75	47	52	64	67

Source: Author's calculations based on 2012 National Asian American Survey.

Note: Data are weighted. Same sizes: white evangelical, n = 42; white non-evangelical, n = 171; black non-evangelical, n = 91; Latinx evangelical, n = 31; Latinx non-evangelical, n = 72; Asian American evangelical, n = 482; Asian American non-evangelical, n = 1,982.

Table A2.2 *Differences in Policy Positions of Born-Again Identifiers, by Race, 2016*

Predicted Probabilities (n = 1,253)	White	Black	Difference
Agrees that a ban on same-sex marriage is needed	38%	38%	0%
Voted for Trump in 2016[a]	40	7	−33
Agrees that immigrants hurt the economy	38	23	−15
Disagrees that the federal government should combat climate change	17	10	−7
Disagrees that taxes on the wealthy should be increased	14	8	−6
Disagrees with more federal funding to aid the poor	10	4	−6
Disagrees that the United States should apologize for slavery	41	14	−27
Opposes the Black Lives Matter movement	25	7	−18

Predicted Probabilities (n = 768)	White	Latinx	Difference
Agrees that a ban on same-sex marriage is needed	43%	42%	−1%
Voted for Trump in 2016[b]	64	39	−25
Agrees that immigrants hurt the economy	42	26	−16
Disagrees that the federal government should combat climate change	17	12	−5
Disagrees that taxes on the wealthy should be increased	20	16	−4
Disagrees with more federal funding to aid the poor	20	8	−12
Disagrees that the United States should apologize for slavery	45	32	−13
Opposes the Black Lives Matter movement	35	21	−14

Predicted Probabilities (n = 677)	White	Asian American	Difference
Agrees that a ban on same-sex marriage is needed	42%	38%	-4%
Voted for Trump in 2016[c]	79	36	-43
Agrees that immigrants hurt the economy	37	26	-11
Disagrees that the federal government should combat climate change	16	9	-7
Disagrees that taxes on the wealthy should be increased	23	13	-10
Disagrees with more federal funding to aid the poor	18	11	-7
Disagrees that the United States should apologize for slavery	47	30	-17
Opposes the Black Lives Matter movement	36	21	-15

Source: Author's calculations based on 2016 CMPS.

[a] Trump vote among voters only: n = 880.

[b] Trump vote among voters only: n = 491.

[c] Trump vote among voters only: n = 380.

Table A2.3 Policy Positions of Evangelicals and Non-evangelicals from Latinx and Asian American National-Origin Subgroups, 2016

Group (n)	Voted for Trump in 2016	Group (n)	Voted for Trump 2016
Chinese evangelical (114)	46%	Mexican evangelical (163)	32%
Chinese non-evangelical (373)	19	Mexican non-evangelical (579)	10
Indian evangelical (23)	29	Central American evangelical (33)	30
Indian non-evangelical (127)	14	Central American non-evangelical (60)	18
Korean evangelical (34)	17		
Korean non-evangelical (60)	13		
Filipino evangelical (18)	51		
Filipino non-evangelical (108)	24		

Group (n)	Disagrees That the Federal Government Should Combat Climate Change	Group (n)	Disagrees That the Federal Government Should Combat Climate Change
Chinese evangelical (156)	12%	Mexican evangelical (288)	12%
Chinese non-evangelical (578)	6	Mexican non-evangelical (956)	7
Indian evangelical (71)	5	Central American evangelical (50)	4
Indian non-evangelical (368)	2	Central American non-evangelical (96)	4
Korean evangelical (72)	11		
Korean non-evangelical (105)	4		
Filipino evangelical (72)	5		
Filipino non-evangelical (309)	5		

	Disagrees with Increasing Taxes on the Wealthy[a]		Disagrees with Increasing Taxes on the Wealthy[a]
Chinese evangelical	8%	Mexican evangelical	13%
Chinese non-evangelical	5	Mexican non-evangelical	7
Indian evangelical	5	Central American evangelical	24
Indian non-evangelical	4	Central American non-evangelical	9
Korean evangelical	11		
Korean non-evangelical	6		
Filipino evangelical	13		
Filipino non-evangelical	9		

Source: Author's calculations based on 2016 CMPS.

[a]Sample sizes same as for analysis of positions on climate change.

NOTES

Chapter 1: Immigration, Religion, and Conservative Politics in the United States

1. Kromm 2015.
2. Jones 2016b.
3. McCaskill 2016.
4. See, for instance, Pieper and Henderson 2017.
5. Smith and Martinez 2016. On evangelicals' demographic decline, see, for instance, Jones 2016a.
6. David Silver, director, Center for Evaluation and Equity Studies, RTI International, unpublished analysis.
7. On rural voters, see Leonard (2017); on Rust Belt voters, see Brownstein (2016); on disaffected white men, see Draut (2017).
8. Olson 2012, 105; see also Layman 2001.
9. Putnam and Campbell 2010; Campbell and Putnam 2012, 24.
10. Smidt 1987.
11. Smidt 2007, 33–34, 47. Although Smidt does suggest in his conclusion that growing numbers of Latinos and Asian Americans could affect voting and issue cohesion among evangelical Protestants, this possibility is not part of his analysis.
12. Wilcox and Robinson 2010; Jelen and Chandler 1996.
13. Smith et al. 1998.
14. Fowler et al. 2010, 35. On evangelicals who identify with the left, see Gasaway 2014. We have learned much about the role of evangelicals in American politics from examinations of the links between religious affiliation and political attitudes. Laura Olson and John Green (2006) and Robert Putnam and David Campbell (2010) provide excellent syntheses of the literature. See also Noll 2001, 2008; Wilson 2007.
15. On the preference for immigrants from northern Europe, see Card (2005) and Masuoka and Junn (2013). Jane Junn (2007) provides a history of restrictions on Asian migration.
16. FitzGerald, Cook-Martin, and García 2014.
17. Card 2005, 301.

18. Holland 2016.
19. Mollenkopf and Hochschild 2010; Lien 1994, 2001, 2004.
20. Pew Research Center 2012a. For the purposes of this book, the term "Asian American" refers to any individual of Asian origin residing in the United States on a permanent or semi-permanent basis regardless of citizenship status. Similarly, "Latinx" refers to individuals of Latin American origin residing in the United States, regardless of citizenship status. European Americans are referred to as "white," and do not include Latinx Americans. Those of African origin are referred to as "black," and, again, do not include those who identify as Latinx. Although it is true that Asian Americans constitute a racial group, or a group shaped by the concept of race, my understanding of race is that it is "a concept that signifies and symbolizes sociopolitical conflicts and interests in reference to different types of human bodies" (Omi and Winant 1994, 55). Thus, the terms "Asian American" and "Asian" represent racial categories, not "races" per se. In a similar respect, the categories of "white," "black," and "Latinx" have been created through social, historical, and political interactions, including state and institutional, as well as local and individual, efforts to organize and redistribute resources by reference to different types of physical features. See also Lopez and Espiritu 1990; Okamoto 2014.
21. Wilcox and Jelen 1990; Layman and Carmines 1997.
22. See, for instance, Layman and Green (2006) and Campbell and Monson (2008).
23. Portes and Rumbaut 2001, 2014; Alba and Nee 2009; Hochschild and Mollenkopf 2009; Bloemraad 2006; Masuoka 2006, 2007. However, see Jones-Correa and Leal (2001), Kelly and Kelly (2005), Ecklund and Park (2005, 2007), Espinosa, Elizondo, and Miranda (2005); and Valenzuela (2014). For excellent studies of Latinx and Asian American religion, see Carnes and Yang (2004a, 2004b), Chen (2008), and Taylor, Gershon, and Pantoja (2014). For excellent studies of post-1965 immigration and politics, see de Graauw (2016), Frasure-Yokley (2015), Gerstle and Mollenkopf (2001), and Brown (2016).
24. Smidt 2007, 47; see also Marti 2009, 2010, 2017.
25. Gonzalez 2007; Streeter 2014.
26. Kim 2006, 2–3; see also Kim 2004.
27. Chuang 2007.
28. Fuller Theological Seminary 2013. After a change in leadership, the Asian American Initiative is now known as the Asian American Center.
29. Graham 2015.
30. Pew Research Center 2015, 53.
31. Putnam and Campbell 2010, 34.
32. PRRI's American Values Atlas is available at http://ava.publicreligion.org/ (accessed January 11, 2018).
33. Jones 2016a.
34. See also Barreto et al. 2018.
35. For 2015 ACS data profiles, see American Community Survey, https://www.census.gov/acs/www/data/data-tables-and-tools/data-profiles/2015/ (accessed January 11, 2018).
36. Foley and Hoge 2007.

37. Seidman 1991.

38. Bebbington 1989; Smidt 2007.

39. Pentecostalism emphasizes the direct experience of God, the ability of the Holy Spirit to inhabit the body, and gifts of the Holy Spirit (Robbins 2004, 117). These gifts may include speaking in tongues and healing. A distinguishing feature of Pentecostalism is "enthusiastic worship"; at services it is not uncommon to witness congregants singing, dancing, crying, shouting, and otherwise demonstrating the rapture of being "moved by the spirit." Major Pentecostal denominations include the Assemblies of God, the Church of God in Christ, and the Foursquare Church (Robbins 2004, 121). Pentecostal worshipers almost always describe themselves as "born-again" or "evangelical" Christians as well. In the 1960s, members of mainline Protestant churches began to experience the "gifts of the spirit" and adopted some of the beliefs and practices of the Pentecostal movement (Robbins 2004, 121).

40. Smidt 2007, 33.

41. For the purpose of this study, the key distinction is between those who self-identify as a "born-again" or "evangelical" Christian, including Catholics, and those who do not so identify themselves. Catholics who identify as born-again or evangelical are a minority (about 10 percent) among all U.S. Catholics, but about one-third of Latino Catholics and one-tenth of Asian American Catholics describe themselves this way. Catholics who identify as born-again—often termed "Charismatic" or "Renewalist"—not only claim to have accepted Jesus as their personal savior (Bebbington 1989), but often adopt practices associated with Pentecostalism, including the intense emotional experiences attributed to being "filled with the spirit," while maintaining ties to the Catholic Church (Pew Research Center 2007; Bishop and Hinojosa 2014).

42. Marty 2011; Green et al. 1996; Evans 2009.

43. Smidt 2007.

44. McVicar 2016, 6.

45. McVicar 2016, 6–7; see also Balmer 2014.

46. Smidt 2007.

47. Pew Research Center 2015.

48. Smidt 2007, 38.

49. Pew Research Center 2015.

50. Smidt 2007, 38; Pew Research Center 2015.

51. Jones 2016a.

52. Lugo and Pond 2007; Jones, Cox, and Navarro-Rivera 2013; Pew Research Center 2015.

53. Author's calculations using Ramakrishnan et al. (2012) and Pew Research Center (2012b, 45).

54. Pew Research Center 2015, 52.

55. Roozen 2013.

56. Brint and Abrutyn 2010; Brooks and Manza 1997; Leege et al. 2002.

57. Wuthnow 1989; Hunter 1991.

58. Davis and Robinson 1996, 243.

59. Davis and Robinson 1996, 343.

60. Smith 2000; Farrell 2011; Bean 2014.
61. McConkey 2001; Gasaway 2014; Ecklund et al. 2017.
62. Merritt 2013.
63. Dias 2013; Jones, Cox, and Navarro-Rivera 2013. For a discussion of the importance of church attendance, see Campbell and Putnam (2012), 35.

Chapter 2: Racial Divides in Evangelical Politics

1. Lugo and Pond 2007, 3.
2. See also Jones, Cox, and Navarro-Rivera (2013) for a comprehensive study of Latino religious identity and political orientations.
3. Barreto et al. 2017.
4. Note that approximately 40 percent of individuals on registered voter lists provide an email address. Barreto et al. 2018.
5. Barreto et al. 2018.
6. The major bias with the 2016 CMPS is that the Asian American sample includes more U.S.-born individuals than other reputable survey samples of Asian Americans. Traditional telephone surveys are biased in the other direction. They tend to include more foreign-born than the actual population. I present data from both an Internet survey (2016 CMPS) and two telephone surveys in the analyses in this chapter. The data are weighted to known population parameters to address sampling biases to the extent possible. See Barreto et al. (2018) for comparisons with other datasets using alternative data collection methods.
7. Berry, Chouhoud, and Junn 2015.
8. Putnam and Campbell 2010; Pew Research Center 2014.
9. Greeley and Hout 2008; Lugo and Pond 2007; Pew Research Center 2011, 2012a, 2014. It is important to note here that attendance at religious services and religious affiliation are related but distinct concepts. Although a majority of those who identify as born-again tend to attend religious services frequently, those who attend religious services at least weekly do not always or even mostly identify as born-again or evangelical. Among the sample as a whole, for example, half of those who identify as born-again also claimed to attend religious services at least once a week. At the same time, only about half of those who reported attending religious services at least once a week also identified as evangelical or born-again.
10. Hankins 2009; Lewis and de Bernardo 2010; Brooks and Manza 1997; Hillygus and Shields 2005; Wilcox and Robinson 2006; Olson, Cadge, and Harrison 2006; Sherkat, De Vries, and Creek 2010. Note that although younger white evangelicals are more liberal on some political attitudes than their older counterparts (Zobgy 2016), they have remained conservative with regard to anti-abortion positions (Cox 2007; Cox and Jones 2015).
11. According to its website (http://blacklivesmatter.com/about/), Black Lives Matter is "a chapter-based national organization working for the validity of Black life. We are working to (re)build the Black liberation movement." For survey question wording, see Latino Decisions, 2016 CMPS, www.latinodecisions.com/

files/1714/8790/9745/CMPS_MASTER_INSTRUMENT.pdf (accessed January 11, 2018).

12. Kim 2010, 128.
13. See also Ellison, Acevedo, and Ramos-Wada 2011.
14. A full methodological description of the 2008 CMPS is available from Barreto et al. 2014 (ICPSR data repository).
15. Wong 2015; see also Wong 2014.
16. Respondents were allowed to select more than one racial group identification. For purposes of this analysis and sampling, 21 respondents who identified with more than one race were classified as white (total white sample n = 1,035); 200 respondents were also classified as Latinx (total Latinx sample n = 3,003); and 60 were classified as black. However, the data do allow us to identify the racial groups selected by those who chose more than one group.
17. For full results, see Wong 2015.
18. Oboler 1995; Kitano and Daniels 2000; Zhou, Ocampo, and Gatewood 2016; Umaña-Taylor, Diversi, and Fine 2002; Jackson et al. 2004.
19. Wong 2014.
20. Smith and Johnson 2010.
21. Putnam 2010.
22. Pew Research Center 2012a, 84.

Chapter 3: Community Boundaries and Perceptions of In-group Embattlement: The Mechanisms Driving Variations in Political Attitudes Among Evangelicals

1. Jones 2016a.
2. Bean 2014.
3. For one critique of this dichotomy, see Banting and Kymlicka 2010.
4. Bean 2014, 218.
5. Bean 2014, 87.
6. Bean 2014, 90.
7. Bean 2014, 119.
8. Bean 2014, 82.
9. Bean 2014, 79.
10. Theiss-Morse 2009, xiii.
11. Theiss-Morse 2009, 64.
12. Theiss-Morse 2009, 65.
13. On social identity theory, see Tajfel 1978; Brewer 2003.
14. Pickett and Brewer 2005.
15. Bean 2014, 122.
16. Bean 2014, 224.
17. Bean 2014, 224.
18. Jones et al. 2016, 18.
19. Jones et al. 2016, 18.
20. Jones et al. 2016, 16.

21. Parker and Barreto 2014.
22. Parker and Barreto 2014, 35.
23. Austin 2015; see also Frasure-Yokley 2018.
24. Green 2017.
25. Djupe and Gilbert 2008, 91, 261; see also Huckfeldt and Sprague 1995.
26. Djupe and Gilbert 2008, 261.
27. Djupe and Gilbert 2008, 111. On racial homogeneity in evangelical churches, see Emerson and Smith 2000.
28. Djupe and Gilbert 2008, 261.
29. McKenzie and Rouse 2013, 219.
30. McKenzie and Rouse 2013, 220; see also Marti 2009, 2010.
31. Putnam and Campbell 2010.
32. Leighley and Matsubayashi 2009. For interesting new research exploring Christian nationalism among Latinx, see Guzman-Garcia (2017).
33. Bean 2014.

Chapter 4: Immigration Trends and Evangelical Communities

1. Pew Research Center 2014.
2. Pew Research Center 2007.
3. Pew Research Center 2014.
4. Pew Research Center 2012a.
5. Stetzer 2016.
6. Bean 2014.
7. Smith 2000, 57.
8. Bean and Teles 2015.
9. Quoted in Bean and Teles 2015, 14.
10. Bean 2014.
11. Bean 2014.
12. Chaves and Eagle 2015, 21.
13. Hicks 2014.
14. Alliance Defending Freedom, http://www.adflegal.org/ (accessed January 11, 2018).
15. Hicks 2014.
16. Bean 2014, 15.
17. Bean 2014, 15.
18. Kuo, Malhotra, and Mo 2014; Bedolla and Haynie 2013; Wallace 2012.
19. Dias 2013.
20. Khalid 2016.
21. See, for example, Green et al. 2005.
22. Murray 2012.
23. Lee and Ramakrishnan 2012.
24. Quoted in Chen 2012.
25. See Asian American Survey, January 2012, at Pew Research Center 2012a, 11.
26. Cooperman 2006.
27. Stafford 2006.

28. Rodriguez 2016; Jenkins 2015.
29. Cole 2009.
30. Stafford 2006.
31. World Relief, the humanitarian arm of the National Association of Evangelicals, did sign the letter.
32. Smith 2006.
33. Smith 2006.
34. Kellstedt and Melkonian-Hoover 2015.
35. Green 2014.
36. Green 2014.
37. Jones et al. 2016, 46.
38. Jones et al. 2016, 38.
39. Lochhead 2006; Stafford 2006; Watanabe and Becerra 2006.
40. *Washington Post* Opinions Staff 2016.
41. Quoted in Showalter 2016.
42. Salguero 2010.
43. See also Espinosa 2007.
44. Pew Research Center 2015.
45. Quoted in Green 2014. See also Jones 2016a, 2016b.
46. O'Brien 2013.
47. Christian Broadcasting Network 2013.
48. Martinez 2009.
49. Martinez 2009.
50. Quoted in Stafford 2006.
51. Binder 2016.
52. Green 2016.
53. Salguero 2016.
54. Bogado 2015.
55. Quoted in Bogado 2015.

Chapter 5: Conclusion: The Persistence of the Right in an Era of Demographic Change

1. Ramírez 2013.
2. Cohn and Caumont 2016.
3. Cohn and Caumont 2016; Meyerson 2016.
4. Alba 2016; see also Wong 2006.
5. Frey 2017.
6. CNN 2016; U.S. Census Bureau, "U.S. Census Bureau QuickFacts: United States," https://www.census.gov/quickfacts/ (accessed January 11, 2018).
7. Cohn 2016.
8. O'Sullivan 2016.
9. Frey 2004.
10. Frey 2017.
11. Pew Research Center 2015, 32; CNN 2016.
12. Frey 2017; Megerian 2016; Templon 2016.

13. Savidge 2016.
14. Merling and Baker 2016.
15. Chokshi 2015.
16. Leighley 2001; Wong 2006; Wong et al. 2011; Barreto et al. 2017.
17. Gasaway 2014.
18. Withrow 2016.
19. Withrow 2016.
20. See also Wong 2006.
21. Ryrie 2017.
22. Ryrie 2017; Young 2015.
23. Ryrie 2017; Gershon, Pantoja, and Taylor 2016.
24. Withrow 2016.
25. Wadsworth 2008; Jacobson and Wadsworth 2012.
26. Wadsworth 2008, 312.
27. Wadsworth 2008, 312.
28. Wadsworth 2008, 313.
29. Greeley and Hout 2008, 73.
30. Wadsworth 2008, 313.
31. Crenshaw 1989; Cohen 1999; Strolovitch 2007.
32. However, see Jacobson and Wadsworth 2012.
33. Lamont and Molnár 2002, 167–68.
34. Epstein 1992, 236.
35. Bean 2014.
36. Merino 2011.
37. Epstein 1992, 236.
38. Fiske 2000.
39. Epstein 1992, 232.
40. Epstein 1992, 237.
41. Lamont 2009.
42. Pickett and Brewer 2005.
43. Kefalas 2002, 50.
44. Parker and Barreto 2014; Austin 2015.
45. Jones-Correa and de Graauw 2013.
46. Boorstein 2017.
47. Boorstein 2017.
48. Quoted in Cook 2016.
49. Wong 2015.
50. Gibson and Hare 2012.
51. Portes 1996; Portes and Rumbaut 2001; Jeung 2005; Park 2008; Chen and Jeung 2012; Ramakrishnan 2005; Busto 1996.
52. Ramakrishnan et al. 2016.
53. Knoll 2012; Rouse, Wilkinson, and Garand 2010.
54. Alberta 2016.
55. Cillizza 2016.

REFERENCES

Alba, Richard. 2016. "The Likely Persistence of a White Majority." *American Prospect*, January 11. http://prospect.org/article/likely-persistence-white-majority-0 (accessed January 11, 2018).

Alba, Richard, and Victor Nee. 2009. *Remaking the American Mainstream: Assimilation and Contemporary Immigration.* Cambridge, Mass.: Harvard University Press.

Alberta, Tim. 2016. "Can the GOP Overcome Demographic Change in Red States?" *National Review*, October 31. http://www.nationalreview.com/article/441595/voter-demographics-diversifying-republicans-falling-behind (accessed January 11, 2018).

Austin, Algernon. 2015. *America Is Not Post-racial: Xenophobia, Islamophobia, Racism, and the 44th President.* Santa Barbara, Calif.: Praeger.

Balmer, Randall. 2014. "The Real Origins of the Religious Right." *Politico Magazine*, May 27. http://politi.co/1tn6Viz (accessed January 11, 2018).

Banting, Keith, and Will Kymlicka. 2010. "Canadian Multiculturalism: Global Anxieties and Local Debates." *British Journal of Canadian Studies* 23(1): 43–72. doi: 10.3828/bjcs.2010.3.

Barreto, Matt, Lorrie Frasure-Yokley, Ange-Marie Hancock, Sylvia Manzano, Karthick Ramakrishnan, Ricardo Ramirez, Gabe Sanchez, and Janelle Wong. 2014. "Collaborative Multi-Racial Post-Election Survey (CMPS), 2008." Inter-university Consortium for Political and Social Research (ICPSR), Ann Arbor, Mich. (distributor). doi: 10.3886/ICPSR35163.v1.

Barreto, Matt, Lorrie Frasure-Yokley, Edward D. Vargas, and Janelle Wong. 2017. "Collaborative Multiracial Post-Election Survey (CMPS) 2016: Topline Results by Race." Latino Decisions, Los Angeles. http://www.latinodecisions.com/files/3914/8902/9717/CMPS_Toplines.pdf (accessed January 11, 2018).

———. 2018. "Best Practices in Collecting Online Data with Asian, Black, Latino, and White Respondents: Evidence from the 2016 Collaborative Multiracial Post-Election Survey." *Politics, Groups, and Identities* (published online January 4). doi: 10.1080/21565503.2017.1419433.

Bean, Lydia. 2014. *The Politics of Evangelical Identity: Local Churches and Partisan Divides in the United States and Canada.* Princeton, N.J.: Princeton University Press.

Bean, Lydia, and Steven Teles. 2015. "Spreading the Gospel of Climate Change: An Evangelical Battleground." Strange Bedfellows Series, New America Foundation, Washington, D.C., November. https://www.newamerica.org/documents/1433/Climate_Care.pdf (accessed January 11, 2018).

Bebbington, David W. 1989. *Evangelicalism in Modern Britain: A History from the 1730s to the 1980s.* London: Unwin Hyman.

Bedolla, Lisa García, and Kerry L. Haynie. 2013. "The Obama Coalition and the Future of American Politics." *Politics, Groups, and Identities* 1(1): 128–33. doi:10.1080/21565503.2012.758593.

Berry, Justin A., Youssef Chouhoud, and Jane Junn. 2015. "Reaching Beyond Low-Hanging Fruit." In *The Oxford Handbook of Polling and Survey Methods,* edited by Lonna Rae Atkeson and R. Michael Alvarez. New York: Oxford University Press.

Binder, John. 2016. "Hispanic Pastor Lists Reasons Why He's Pro-Trump and It's Everything the Media Doesn't Want You to See!" *Bizpac Review,* June 21. http://www.bizpacreview.com/2016/06/21/hispanic-pastor-lists-reasons-why-hes-pro-trump-and-its-everything-the-media-doesnt-want-you-to-see-355124 (accessed January 11, 2018).

Bishop, Marlon, and Maria Hinojosa. 2014. "A Different Kind of Catholicism Grows in Latino Communities." *Morning Edition,* NPR, January 23. http://www.npr.org/sections/codeswitch/2014/01/23/262793319/a-different-kind-of-catholicism-grows-in-latino-communities (accessed January 11, 2018).

Bloemraad, Irene. 2006. *Becoming a Citizen: Incorporating Immigrants and Refugees in the United States and Canada.* Berkeley: University of California Press.

Bogado, Aura. 2015. "Latino Evangelicals Push—and Win—on Death Penalty Abolition in Nebraska." *ColorLines,* May 29. http://www.colorlines.com/articles/latino-evangelicals-push%E2%80%94and-win%E2%80%94-death-penalty-abolition-nebraska (accessed January 11, 2018).

Boorstein, Michelle. 2017. "In D.C., White Evangelicals Are Literally the 1 Percent." *Washington Post,* September 6. https://www.washingtonpost.com/news/acts-of-faith/wp/2017/09/06/in-d-c-white-evangelicals-are-literally-the-1-percent/ (accessed January 11, 2018).

Brewer, Marilynn B. 2003. "Optimal Distinctiveness, Social Identity, and the Self." In *Handbook of Self and Identity,* edited by Mark R. Leary and June Price Tangney. New York: Guilford Press.

Brint, Steven, and Seth Abrutyn. 2010. "Who's Right About the Right? Comparing Competing Explanations of the Link Between White Evangelicals and Conservative Politics in the United States." *Journal for the Scientific Study of Religion* 49(2): 328–50. doi:10.1111/j.1468-5906.2010.01513.x.

Brooks, Clem, and Jeff Manza. 1997. "Social Cleavages and Political Alignments: U.S. Presidential Elections, 1960 to 1992." *American Sociological Review* 62(6): 937–46. doi:10.2307/2657348.

Brown, Heath. 2016. *Immigrants and Electoral Politics: Nonprofit Organizing in a Time of Demographic Change.* Ithaca, N.Y.: Cornell University Press.

Brownstein, Ronald. 2016. "How the Rustbelt Paved Trump's Road to Victory." *Atlantic,* November 10. https://www.theatlantic.com/politics/archive/2016/11/trumps-road-to-victory/507203/ (accessed January 11, 2018).

Busto, Rudy. 1996. "The Gospel According to the Model Minority? Hazarding an Interpretation of Asian American Evangelical College Students." *Amerasia Journal* 22(1): 133–47.

Campbell, David E., and J. Quin Monson. 2008. "The Religion Card: Gay Marriage and the 2004 Presidential Election." *Public Opinion Quarterly* 72(3): 399–419. doi:10.1093/poq/nfn032.

Campbell, David E., and Robert D. Putnam. 2012. "God and Caesar in America: Why Mixing Religion and Politics Is Bad for Both." *Foreign Affairs* 91(March/April): 34.

Card, David. 2005. "Is the New Immigration Really So Bad?" *Economic Journal* 115(507): F300–23.

Carnes, Tony, and Fenggang Yang. 2004a. "Introduction." In *Asian American Religions: The Making and Remaking of Borders and Boundaries,* edited by Tony Carnes and Fenggang Yang. New York: New York University Press.

———. eds. 2004b. *Asian American Religions: The Making and Remaking of Borders and Boundaries.* New York: New York University Press.

Chaves, Mark, and Alison Eagle. 2015. "Religious Congregations in 21st Century America: National Congregations Study." Duke University, Durham, N.C. http://www.soc.duke.edu/natcong/Docs/NCSIII_report_final.pdf (accessed January 11, 2018).

Chen, Caroline. 2012. "Why Do Asian Americans Vote for Democrats?" December 3. http://www.huffingtonpost.com/caroline-chen/asian-american-voters_b_2231418.html (accessed January 11, 2018).

Chen, Carolyn. 2008. *Getting Saved in America: Taiwanese Immigration and Religious Experience.* Princeton, N.J.: Princeton University Press.

Chen, Carolyn, and Russell Jeung, eds. 2012. *Sustaining Faith Traditions: Race, Ethnicity, and Religion Among the Latino and Asian American Second Generation.* New York: New York University Press.

Chokshi, Niraj. 2015. "The Religious States of America, in 22 Maps." *Washington Post,* February 26. https://www.washingtonpost.com/blogs/govbeat/wp/2015/02/26/the-religious-states-of-america-in-22-maps/ (accessed January 11, 2018).

Christian Broadcasting Network. 2013. "Public Checked Out on Immigration Reform Debate." Christian Broadcasting Network, May 8. https://www.youtube.com/watch?v=I68OWRBHRVc (accessed January 11, 2018).

Chuang, D. J. 2007. "Asian American Churches: An Introductory Survey." L2 Foundation and Leadership Network, April. http://leadnet.org/docs/AsianAmer-2007-MAR-Asian_American_Churches_Intro-Chuang.pdf (document no longer available).

Cillizza, Chris. 2016. "The Coming Republican Demographic Disaster, in 1 Stunning Chart." *Washington Post,* April 25. https://www.washingtonpost.com/news/the-fix/wp/2016/04/25/the-coming-republican-demographic-disaster-in-1-stunning-chart/ (accessed January 11, 2018).

CNN. 2016. "Exit Polls 2016." *CNN Politics,* November 23. http://edition.cnn.com/election/results/exit-polls.

Cohen, Cathy J. 1999. *The Boundaries of Blackness: AIDS and the Breakdown of Black Politics.* Chicago: University of Chicago Press.

Cohn, D'vera, and Rea Caumont. 2016. "10 Demographic Trends That Are Shaping the U.S. and the World." Pew Research Center, Washington, D.C., March 31. http://www.pewresearch.org/fact-tank/2016/03/31/10-demographic-trends-that-are-shaping-the-u-s-and-the-world/ (accessed January 11, 2018).

Cohn, Nate. 2016. "There Are More White Voters Than People Think. That's Good News for Trump." *New York Times,* June 9. https://www.nytimes.com/2016/06/10/upshot/there-are-more-white-voters-than-people-think-thats-good-news-for-trump.html (accessed January 11, 2018).

Cole, Ethan. 2009. "Some Christians Applaud Obama's Push for Immigration Reform." *Christian Post,* April 10. http://www.christianpost.com/news/some-christians-applaud-obama-s-push-for-immigration-reform-38015/ (accessed January 11, 2018).

Cook, Lindsey. 2016. "The Declining Influence of White Christian America, in Charts." *U.S. News & World Report,* July 19. https://www.usnews.com/news/articles/2016-07-19/the-declining-influence-of-white-christian-america-in-charts (accessed January 11, 2018).

Cooperman, Alan. 2006. "Letter on Immigration Deepens Split Among Evangelicals." *Washington Post,* April 5. http://www.washingtonpost.com/wp-dyn/content/article/2006/04/04/AR2006040401606_pf.html (accessed January 11, 2018).

Cox, Dan. 2007. "Young White Evangelicals: Less Republican, Still Conservative." Religion & Public Life Project, Pew Research Center, Washington, D.C., September 28. http://www.pewforum.org/2007/09/28/young-white-evangelicals-less-republican-still-conservative/ (accessed January 11, 2018).

Cox, Dan, and Robert Jones. 2015. "How Race and Religion Shape Millennial Attitudes on Sexuality and Reproductive Health." Public Religion Research Institute, Washington, D.C., March 27. http://www.prri.org/research/survey-how-race-and-religion-shape-millennial-attitudes-on-sexuality-and-reproductive-health/ (accessed January 11, 2018).

Crenshaw, Kimberlé. 1989. "Demarginalizing the Intersection of Race and Sex: A Black Feminist Critique of Antidiscrimination Doctrine, Feminist Theory, and Antiracist Politics." *University of Chicago Legal Forum* 1: 139.

Davis, Nancy, and Robert Robinson. 1996. "Rejoinder to Hunter: Religious Orthodoxy: An Army Without Foot Soldiers?" *Journal for the Scientific Study of Religion* 35(3): 249–51.

de Graauw, Els. 2016. *Making Immigrant Rights Real: Nonprofits and the Politics of Integration in San Francisco.* Ithaca, N.Y.: Cornell University Press.

Dias, Elizabeth. 2013. "Evangelicos: A Way Back for the GOP." *Time,* April 8. http://swampland.time.com/2013/04/08/evangelicos-a-way-back-for-the-gop/ (accessed January 11, 2018).

Djupe, Paul A., and Christopher P. Gilbert. 2008. *The Political Influence of Churches*. New York: Cambridge University Press.

Draut, Tamara. 2016. "The New Working Class: Trump Can Talk to Disaffected White Men, but They Don't Make Up the 'Working Class' Anymore." *Salon*, July 23. http://www.salon.com/2016/07/23/the_new_working_class_trump_can_talk_to_disaffected_white_men_but_they_dont_make_up_the_working_class_anymore_partner/ (accessed January 11, 2018); originally appeared at *billmoyers.com*.

Ecklund, Elaine Howard, and Jerry Z. Park. 2005. "Asian American Community Participation and Religion: Civic Model Minorities?" *Journal of Asian American Studies* 8(1): 1–21. doi:10.1353/jaas.2005.0027.

———. 2007. "Religious Diversity and Community Volunteerism Among Asian Americans." *Journal for the Scientific Study of Religion* 46(2): 233–44. doi:10.1111/j.1468-5906.2007.00353.x.

Ecklund, Elaine Howard, Christopher P. Scheitle, Jared Peifer, and Daniel Bolger. 2017. "Examining Links Between Religion, Evolution Views, and Climate Change Skepticism." *Environment and Behavior* 49(9): 985–1006. doi: 10.1177/0013916516674246.

Ellison, Christopher G., Gabriel A. Acevedo, and Aida I. Ramos-Wada. 2011. "Religion and Attitudes Toward Same-Sex Marriage Among U.S. Latinos." *Social Science Quarterly* 92(1): 35–56. doi: 10.1111/j.1540-6237.2011.00756.x.

Emerson, Michael O., and Christian Smith. 2000. *Divided by Faith: Evangelical Religion and the Problem of Race in America*. New York: Oxford University Press.

Epstein, Cynthia Fuchs. 1992. "Tinkerbells and Pinups: The Construction of Gender and Boundaries at Work." In *Cultivating Differences: Symbolic Boundaries and the Making of Inequality*, edited by Michèle Lamont and Marcel Fournier. Chicago: University of Chicago Press.

Espinosa, Gastón. 2007. "'Today We Act, Tomorrow We Vote': Latino Religions, Politics, and Activism in Contemporary U.S. Civil Society." *Annals of the American Academy of Political and Social Science* 612(1): 152–71. doi: 10.1177/0002716207301099.

Espinosa, Gastón, Virgilio P. Elizondo, and Jesse Miranda. 2005. *Latino Religions and Civic Activism in the United States*. New York: Oxford University Press.

Evans, John. 2009. "Where Is the Counterweight? Explorations of the Decline in Mainline Protestant Participation in Public Debates over Values." In *Evangelicals and Democracy in America: Religion and Politics*, edited by Steven Brint and Jean Reith Schroedel. New York: Russell Sage Foundation.

Farrell, Justin. 2011. "The Young and the Restless? The Liberalization of Young Evangelicals." *Journal for the Scientific Study of Religion* 50(3): 517–32. doi:10.1111/j.1468-5906.2011.01589.x.

Fiske, Susan T. 2000. "Stereotyping, Prejudice, and Discrimination at the Seam Between the Centuries: Evolution, Culture, Mind, and Brain." *European Journal of Social Psychology* 30(2): 299–322.

FitzGerald, David Scott, David Cook-Martin, and Angela S. García. 2014. *Culling the Masses: The Democratic Origins of Racist Immigration in the Americas*. Cambridge, Mass.: Harvard University Press.

Foley, Michael W., and Dean R. Hoge. 2007. *Religion and the New Immigrants: How Faith Communities Form Our Newest Citizens.* New York: Oxford University Press.

Fowler, Robert Booth, Allen D. Hertzke, Laura R. Olson, and Kevin R. Den Dulk. 2010. *Religion and Politics in America: Faith, Culture, and Strategic Choices.* 4th ed. Boulder, Colo.: Westview Press.

Frasure-Yokley, Lorrie. 2015. *Racial and Ethnic Politics in American Suburbs.* New York: Cambridge University Press.

———. 2018. "Choosing the Velvet Glove: Women Voters, Ambivalent Sexism, and Vote Choice in 2016." *Journal of Race, Ethnicity, and Politics* (forthcoming).

Frey, William H. 2004. "Older White Vote Still Powerhouse in White House Contest." Brookings Institution, Washington, D.C., October 24. https://www.brookings. edu/opinions/older-white-vote-still-powerhouse-in-white-house-contest/ (accessed January 11, 2018).

———. 2017. "Census Shows Pervasive Decline in 2016 Minority Voter Turnout." Brookings Institution, Washington, D.C., May 18. https://www.brookings.edu/ blog/the-avenue/2017/05/18/census-shows-pervasive-decline-in-2016-minority-voter-turnout/ (accessed January 11, 2018).

Fuller Theological Seminary. 2013. "Fuller Announces New Asian American Initiative." Fuller Theological Seminary, Pasadena, Calif., September 25. http://fuller. edu/about/news-and-events/articles/2013/fuller-announces-new-asian-american-initiative/ (accessed January 11, 2018).

Gasaway, Brantley W. 2014. *Progressive Evangelicals and the Pursuit of Social Justice.* Chapel Hill: University of North Carolina Press.

Gershon, Sarah Allen, Adrian D. Pantoja, and J. Benjamin Taylor. 2016. "God in the Barrio? The Determinants of Religiosity and Civic Engagement Among Latinos in the United States." *Politics and Religion* 9(1): 84–110. doi:10.1017/ S175504831600002X.

Gerstle, Gary, and John Mollenkopf, eds. 2001. *E Pluribus Unum? Contemporary and Historical Perspectives on Immigrant Political Incorporation.* New York: Russell Sage Foundation.

Gibson, Troy, and Christopher Hare. 2012. "Do Latino Christians and Seculars Fit the Culture War Profile? Latino Religiosity and Political Behavior." *Politics and Religion* 5(1): 53–82. doi: 10.1017/S1755048311000630.

Gonzalez, David. 2007. "A Sliver of a Storefront, a Faith on the Rise." *New York Times,* January 14. www.nytimes.com/2007/01/14/nyregion/14storefront.html (accessed January 11, 2018).

Graham, Stephen. 2015. "2015 State of the Industry Webinar." Association of Theological Schools in the United States and Canada, Pittsburgh, September 18. www.ats.edu/uploads/resources/publications-presentations/ documents/2015-state-of-the-industry-webinar-text.pdf (accessed January 11, 2018).

Greeley, Andrew M., and Michael Hout. 2008. *The Truth About Conservative Christians: What They Think and What They Believe.* Chicago: University of Chicago Press.

Green, Emma. 2014. "The Evangelical Slide on Immigration Reform." *Atlantic,*
June 11. http://www.theatlantic.com/politics/archive/2014/06/the-evangelical-
slide-on-immigration-reform/372541/ (accessed January 11, 2018).

———. 2016. "Trump Appointed His Evangelical Executive Advisory Board."
Atlantic, June 21. http://www.theatlantic.com/politics/archive/2016/06/
trump-is-surrounding-himself-with-evangelical-pastors/488114/ (accessed
January 11, 2018).

———. 2017. "White Evangelicals Believe They Face More Discrimination
Than Muslims." *Atlantic,* March 10. https://www.theatlantic.com/politics/
archive/2017/03/perceptions-discrimination-muslims-christians/519135/
(accessed January 11, 2018).

Green, John Clifford, James L. Guth, Corwin E. Smidt, and Lyman A. Kellstedt.
1996. *Religion and the Culture Wars.* Lanham, Md.: Rowman & Littlefield.

Green, John C., Corwin E. Smidt, James L. Guth, and Lyman A. Kellstedt. 2005.
"The American Religious Landscape and the 2004 Presidential Vote: Increased
Polarization." Pew Research Forum, Pew Research Center, Washington, D.C.
http://www-aws.pewtrusts.org/~/media/legacy/uploadedfiles/wwwpewtrustsorg/
news/press_releases/religion_in_public_life/pewreligionreligiousland020305pdf.
pdf (accessed January 11, 2018).

Guzman-Garcia, Melissa. 2017. "Negotiating Christian Identities in a Xenophobic
World: A Case Study of Mexican Immigrants in Central California." Paper
prepared for California State University, San Francisco, Workshop on Race
and Immigration, December 6.

Hankins, Barry. 2009. *American Evangelicals: A Contemporary History of a Mainstream Religious Movement.* Lanham, Md.: Rowman & Littlefield.

Hicks, Josh. 2014. "Political Pastors Openly Defying IRS Rules on Candidate
Endorsements." *Washington Post,* November 4. https://www.washingtonpost.com/
news/federal-eye/wp/2014/11/04/political-pastors-defying-irs-rules-on-
candidate-endorsements/ (accessed January 11, 2018).

Hillygus, D. Sunshine, and Todd G. Shields. 2005. "Moral Issues and Voter Decision Making in the 2004 Presidential Election." *Political Science and Politics*
38(2): 201–09.

Hochschild, Jennifer L., and John H. Mollenkopf. 2009. *Bringing Outsiders In:
Transatlantic Perspectives on Immigrant Political Incorporation.* Ithaca, N.Y.:
Cornell University Press.

Holland, Jesse. 2016. "Census: Asians Remain Fastest-Growing Racial Group in
U.S." Associated Press, June 23. https://apnews.com/544b8c3d65394c17b
960518d39eb96e9/census-asians-remain-fastest-growing-racial-group-us
(accessed January 11, 2018).

Huckfeldt, R. Robert, and John Sprague. 1995. *Citizens, Politics, and Social Communication: Information and Influence in an Election Campaign.* New York:
Cambridge University Press.

Hunter, James Davison. 1991. *Culture Wars: The Struggle to Control the Family, Art,
Education, Law, and Politics in America.* New York: Basic Books.

Jackson, James S., Myriam Torres, Cleopatra H. Caldwell, Harold W. Neighbors, Randolph M. Nesse, Robert Joseph Taylor, Steven J. Trierweiler, and David R. Williams. 2004. "The National Survey of American Life: A Study of Racial, Ethnic, and Cultural Influences on Mental Disorders and Mental Health." *International Journal of Methods in Psychiatric Research* 13(4): 196–207. doi: 10.1002/mpr.177.

Jacobson, Robin Dale, and Nancy D. Wadsworth. 2012. *Faith and Race in American Political Life.* Charlottesville: University of Virginia Press.

Jelen, Ted G., and Marthe A. Chandler. 1996. "Patterns of Religious Socialization: Communalism, Associationalism, and the Politics of Lifestyle." *Review of Religious Research* 38(2): 142–58. doi:10.2307/3512338.

Jenkins, Jack. 2015. "The Explosive Growth of Evangelical Belief in Latinos Has Big Political Implications." *ThinkProgress,* June 16. http://thinkprogress.org/politics/2015/06/16/3668780/hispanic-evangelicals-battle-political-soul-americas-curious-new-swing-vote/ (accessed January 11, 2018).

Jeung, Russell. 2005. *Faithful Generations: Race and New Asian American Churches.* New Brunswick, N.J.: Rutgers University Press.

Jones, Robert P. 2016a. *The End of White Christian America.* New York: Simon & Schuster.

———. 2016b. "Southern Evangelicals: Dwindling—and Taking the GOP Edge with Them." *Atlantic,* October 17. http://www.theatlantic.com/politics/archive/2014/10/the-shriking-evangelical-voter-pool/381560/ (accessed January 11, 2018).

Jones, Robert, Dan Cox, and Juhem Navarro-Rivera. 2013. "How Shifting Religious Identities and Experiences Are Influencing Hispanic Approaches to Politics." Public Religion Research Institute, Washington, D.C., September 27. http://www.prri.org/research/hispanic-values-survey-2013/ (accessed January 11, 2018).

Jones, Robert, Daniel Cox, E. J. Dionne, William Galston, Betsy Cooper, and Rachel Lienesch. 2016. "How Immigration and Concerns About Cultural Changes Are Shaping the 2016 Election: Findings from the 2016 PRRI/Brookings Immigration Survey." Public Religion Research Institute, Washington, D.C., June 23. https://www.brookings.edu/wp-content/uploads/2016/06/20160623_prri_jones_presentation.pdf (accessed January 11, 2018).

Jones-Correa, Michael A., and David L. Leal. 2001. "Political Participation: Does Religion Matter?" *Political Research Quarterly* 54(4): 751–70. doi:10.1177/106591290105400404.

Jones-Correa, Michael, and Els de Graauw. 2013. "Looking Back to See Ahead: Unanticipated Changes in Immigration from 1986 to the Present and Their Implications for American Politics Today." *Annual Review of Political Science* 16(1): 209–30. doi: 10.1146/annurev-polisci-051211-164644.

Junn, Jane. 2007. "From Coolie to Model Minority: U.S. Immigration Policy and the Construction of Racial Identity." *Du Bois Review: Social Science Research on Race* (September). doi:10.1017/S1742058X07070208.

Kefalas, Marla. 2002. "Chicago's Last Garden Spot." *Contexts* 1(3): 50–55. http://journals.sagepub.com/doi/abs/10.1525/ctx.2002.1.3.50 (accessed January 11, 2018).

Kellstedt, Lyman A., and Ruth Melkonian-Hoover. 2015. "White Evangelicals and Immigration Reform." *Christian Post,* February 6. http://www.christianpost. com/news/white-evangelicals-and-immigration-reform-133687/ (accessed January 11, 2018).

Kelly, Nathan J., and Jana Morgan Kelly. 2005. "Religion and Latino Partisanship in the United States." *Political Research Quarterly* 58(1): 87–95. doi:10.1177/106591290505800108.

Khalid, Asma. 2016. "Latinos Will Never Vote for a Republican, and Other Myths About Hispanics from 2016." *Morning Edition,* NPR, December 22. https://www.npr.org/2016/12/22/506347254/latinos-will-never-vote-for-a-republican-and-other-myths-about-hispanics-from-20 (accessed January 11, 2018).

Kim, Rebecca Y. 2004. "Second-Generation Korean American Evangelicals: Ethnic, Multiethnic, or White Campus Ministries?" *Sociology of Religion* 65(1): 19–34.

———. 2006. *God's New Whiz Kids? Korean American Evangelicals on Campus.* New York: New York University Press.

Kim, Sharon. 2010. *A Faith of Our Own: Second-Generation Spirituality in Korean American Churches.* Newark, N.J.: Rutgers University Press.

Kitano, Harry H. L., and Roger Daniels. 2000. *Asian Americans: Emerging Minorities.* 3rd ed. Upper Saddle River, N.J.: Pearson.

Knoll, Benjamin R. 2012. "¿Compañero o Extranjero? Anti-immigrant Nativism Among Latino Americans." *Social Science Quarterly* 93(4): 911–31. doi:10.1111/j.1540-6237.2012.00872.x.

Krogstad, Jens Manuel, and Mark Hugo Lopez. 2017. "Black Voter Turnout Fell in 2016, Even as a Record Number of Americans Cast Ballots." Pew Research Center, Washington, D.C., May 12. http://www.pewresearch.org/fact-tank/2017/05/12/black-voter-turnout-fell-in-2016-even-as-a-record-number-of-americans-cast-ballots/ (accessed January 11, 2018).

Kromm, Chris. 2015. "How the Decline of Southern White Evangelicals Fuels the Passage of 'Religious Freedom' Laws." *American Prospect,* April 21. http://prospect.org/article/how-decline-southern-white-evangelicals-fuels-passage-religious-freedom-laws.

Kuo, Alexander, Neil A. Malhotra, and Cecilia Hyunjung Mo. 2014. "Why Do Asian Americans Identify as Democrats? Testing Theories of Social Exclusion and Intergroup Solidarity." SSRN Scholarly Paper ID 2423950, Social Science Research Network, Rochester, N.Y., February 25. http://papers.ssrn.com/abstract=2423950 (accessed January 11, 2018).

Lamont, Michèle. 2009. "Responses to Racism, Health, and Social Inclusion as a Dimension of Successful Societies." In *Successful Societies: How Institutions and Culture Affect Health,* edited by Peter A. Hall and Michèle Lamont. New York: Cambridge University Press.

Lamont, Michèle, and Virág Molnár. 2002. "The Study of Boundaries in the Social Sciences." *Annual Review of Sociology* 28(1): 167–95. doi:10.1146/annurev.soc.28.110601.141107.

Layman, Geoffrey. 2001. *The Great Divide: Religious and Cultural Conflict in American Party Politics.* New York: Columbia University Press.

Layman, Geoffrey C., and Edward G. Carmines. 1997. "Cultural Conflict in American Politics: Religious Traditionalism, Postmaterialism, and U.S. Political Behavior." *Journal of Politics* 59(3): 751–77. doi:10.2307/2998636.

Layman, Geoffrey C., and John C. Green. 2006. "Wars and Rumours of Wars: The Contexts of Cultural Conflict in American Political Behaviour." *British Journal of Political Science* 36(1): 61–89. doi:10.1017/S0007123406000044.

Lee, Taeku, and Karthick Ramakrishnan. 2012. "Asian Americans Vote Democratic." *Los Angeles Times,* November 23. http://articles.latimes.com/2012/nov/23/opinion/la-oe-lee-asian-american-voters-20121123 (accessed January 11, 2018).

Leege, David C., Kenneth D. Wald, Paul D. Mueller, and Brian S. Krueger. 2002. *The Politics of Cultural Differences: Social Change and Voter Mobilization Strategies in the Post–New Deal Period.* Princeton, N.J.: Princeton University Press.

Leighley, Jan E. 2001. *Strength in Numbers? The Political Mobilization of Racial and Ethnic Minorities.* Princeton, N.J.: Princeton University Press.

Leighley, Jan E., and Tetsuya Matsubayashi. 2009. "The Implications of Class, Race, and Ethnicity for Political Networks." *American Politics Research* 37(5): 824–55.

Leonard, Robert. 2017. "Why Rural America Voted for Trump." *New York Times,* January 5. https://www.nytimes.com/2017/01/05/opinion/why-rural-america-voted-for-trump.html?_r=0 (accessed January 11, 2018).

Lewis, Andrew R., and Dana Huyser de Bernardo. 2010. "Belonging Without Belonging: Utilizing Evangelical Self-Identification to Analyze Political Attitudes and Preferences." *Journal for the Scientific Study of Religion* 49(1): 112–26.

Lien, Pei-te. 1994. "Ethnicity and Political Participation: A Comparison Between Asian and Mexican Americans." *Political Behavior* 16(2): 237–64. doi:10.1007/BF01498879.

———. 2001. *The Making of Asian America Through Political Participation.* Philadelphia: Temple University Press.

———. 2004. "Asian Americans and Voting Participation: Comparing Racial and Ethnic Differences in Recent U.S. Elections." *International Migration Review* 38(2): 493–517.

Lochhead, Carolyn. 2006. "Immigration Debate Splits Christian Right." *SFGate,* April 28. http://www.sfgate.com/politics/article/Immigration-debate-splits-Christian-right-2498370.php (accessed January 11, 2018).

Lopez, David, and Yen Espiritu. 1990. "Panethnicity in the United States: A Theoretical Framework." *Ethnic and Racial Studies* 13(2): 198–224.

Lugo, Luis, and Allison Pond. 2007. "¡Here Come 'Los Evangélicos'!" Pew Forum on Religion and Public Life, Pew Research Center, Washington, D.C., June 6. http://www.pewforum.org/2007/06/06/here-come-los-evanglicos/ (accessed January 11, 2018).

Marti, Gerardo. 2009. *A Mosaic of Believers: Diversity and Innovation in a Multiethnic Church.* Bloomington: Indiana University Press.

———. 2010. "The Religious Racial Integration of African Americans into Diverse Churches." *Journal for the Scientific Study of Religion* 49(2): 201–17.

———. 2017. *Worship Across the Racial Divide: Religious Music and the Multiracial Congregation.* New York: Oxford University Press.

Martinez, Gebe. 2009. "Gay Partner Verbiage Could Kill Reform." *Politico,* June 3. http://www.politico.com/story/2009/06/gay-partner-verbiage-could-kill-reform-023262 (accessed January 11, 2018).

Marty, Martin E., ed. 2011. *Fundamentalism and Evangelicalism.* Vol. 10, *Modern American Protestantism and Its World.* Berlin: Walter de Gruyter & Co. First published 1993 by K. G. Saur (Munich).

Masuoka, Natalie. 2006. "Together They Become One: Examining the Predictors of Panethnic Group Consciousness Among Asian Americans and Latinos." *Social Science Quarterly* 87(5): 993–1011. doi:10.1111/j.1540-6237.2006.00412.x.

———. 2007. "Defining the Group: Latino Identity and Political Participation." *American Politics Research* 36(1). doi:10.1177/1532673X07303936.

Masuoka, Natalie, and Jane Junn. 2013. *The Politics of Belonging: Race, Public Opinion, and Immigration.* Chicago: University of Chicago Press.

McCaskill, Nolan D. 2016. "Trump Tells Wisconsin: Victory Was a Surprise." *Politico,* December 13. http://politi.co/2hjRGeU (accessed January 11, 2018).

McConkey, Dale. 2001. "Whither Hunter's Culture War? Shifts in Evangelical Morality, 1988–1998." *Sociology of Religion* 62(2): 149–74. doi: 10.2307/3712453.

McKenzie, Brian D., and Stella M. Rouse. 2013. "Shades of Faith: Religious Foundations of Political Attitudes Among African Americans, Latinos, and Whites." *American Journal of Political Science* 57(1): 218–35. doi:10.1111/j.1540-5907.2012.00611.x.

McVicar, Michael J. 2016. "The Religious Right in America." *The Oxford Research Encyclopedia of Religion* (March). doi: 10.1093/acrefore/9780199340378.013.97.

Megerian, Chris. 2016. "These Battleground States Will Decide Our Next President." *Los Angeles Times,* October 13, updated November 1, 2016. http://www.latimes.com/projects/la-na-pol-battleground-state-cheat-sheet/ (accessed January 11, 2018).

Merino, Stephen M. 2011. "Neighbors Like Me? Religious Affiliation and Neighborhood Racial Preferences Among Non-Hispanic Whites." *Religions* 2(2): 165–83. doi:10.3390/rel2020165.

Merling, Lara, and Dean Baker. 2016. "In the Electoral College White Votes Matter More." *Beat the Press* (blog). Center for Economic and Policy Research, Washington, D.C., November 13. http://cepr.net/blogs/beat-the-press/in-the-electoral-college-white-votes-matter-more.

Merritt, Jonathan. 2013. "The Rise of the Christian Left in America." *Atlantic,* July 25. https://www.theatlantic.com/politics/archive/2013/07/the-rise-of-the-christian-left-in-america/278086/ (accessed January 11, 2018).

Meyerson, Harold. 2016. "Yes, but How Will They Vote?" *American Prospect,* February 11, http://prospect.org/article/yes-how-will-they-vote (accessed January 11, 2018).

Mollenkopf, John, and Jennifer Hochschild. 2010. "Immigrant Political Incorporation: Comparing Success in the United States and Western Europe." *Ethnic and Racial Studies* 33(1):19–38. doi: 10.1080/01419870903197373.

Murray, Charles. 2012. "Why Aren't Asians Republicans?" American Enterprise Institute, Washington, D.C., November 26. https://www.aei.org/publication/why-arent-asians-republicans/ (accessed January 11, 2018).

Noll, Mark A. 2001. *American Evangelical Christianity: An Introduction.* Malden, Mass.: Blackwell Publishers.

———. 2008. "Protestant Evangelicals and Recent American Politics." *Journal of American and Canadian Studies* 25: 3–18.

Oboler, Suzanne. 1995. *Ethnic Labels, Latino Lives: Identity and the Politics of (Re)Presentation in the United States.* Minneapolis: University of Minnesota Press.

O'Brien, Matt. 2013. "Same-Sex Couples Would Get a Break in Rep. Honda's Immigrant Measure." *San Jose Mercury News,* August 12. http://www.mercurynews.com/ci_22599345/immigrant-same-sex-couples-would-get-break-rep (accessed January 11, 2018).

Okamoto, Dina G. 2014. *Redefining Race: Asian American Panethnicity and Shifting Ethnic Boundaries.* New York: Russell Sage Foundation.

Olson, Laura R. 2012. "Religion and American Public Life." *Perspectives on Politics* 10(1): 103–06.

Olson, Laura R., Wendy Cadge, and James T. Harrison. 2006. "Religion and Public Opinion about Same-Sex Marriage." *Social Science Quarterly* 87(2): 340–60. doi:10.1111/j.1540-6237.2006.00384.x.

Olson, Laura R., and John C. Green. 2006. "The Religion Gap." *PS: Political Science and Politics* 39(3): 455–59. doi:10.1017/S1049096506060860.

Omi, Michael, and Howard Winant. 1994. *Racial Formation in the United States: From the 1960s to the 1990s.* London: Routledge.

O'Sullivan, John. 2016. "The Latino Voting Surge That Never Happened." *National Review,* November 22. http://www.nationalreview.com/article/442384/hispanic-turnout-disappoints-democrats-undermines-permanent-majority-theory; Krogstad and Lopez 2017 (accessed January 11, 2018).

Park, Jerry Z. 2008. "Second-Generation Asian American Pan-Ethnic Identity: Pluralized Meanings of a Racial Label." *Sociological Perspectives* 51(3): 541–61. doi:10.1525/sop.2008.51.3.541.

Parker, Christopher S., and Matt A. Barreto. 2014. *Change They Can't Believe In: The Tea Party and Reactionary Politics in America.* Princeton, N.J.: Princeton University Press.

Pew Research Center. 2007. "Changing Faiths: Latinos and the Transformation of American Religion." Pew Forum on Hispanic Trends, Pew Research Center, Washington, D.C., April 25. http://www.pewhispanic.org/2007/04/25/changing-faiths-latinos-and-the-transformation-of-american-religion/ (accessed January 11, 2018).

———. 2011. "Evangelical Beliefs and Practices." Pew Forum on Religion & Public Life, Pew Research Center, Washington, D.C., June 22. http://www.pewforum.org/2011/06/22/global-survey-beliefs/ (accessed January 11, 2018).

————. 2012a. "The Rise of Asian Americans." Pew Forum on Social & Demographic Trends, Pew Research Center, Washington, D.C., June 19. http://www.pewsocialtrends.org/2012/06/19/the-rise-of-asian-americans/ (accessed January 11, 2018).

————. 2012b. "Asian Americans: A Mosaic of Faiths." Pew Forum on Religion and Public Life, Pew Research Center, Washington, D.C., July 19. http://www.pewforum.org/2012/07/19/asian-americans-a-mosaic-of-faiths-overview/ (accessed January 11, 2018).

————. 2014. *The Shifting Religious Identity of Latinos in the United States.* Religion & Public Life Project, Pew Research Center, Washington, D.C., May 7. http://www.pewforum.org/files/2014/05/Latinos-Religion-07-22-full-report.pdf (accessed January 11, 2018).

————. 2015. "America's Changing Religious Landscape" (the *2014 U.S. Religious Landscape Study*). Religion & Public Life Project, Pew Research Center, Washington, D.C., May 12. http://www.pewforum.org/2015/05/12/americas-changing-religious-landscape/ (accessed January 11, 2018).

Pickett, Cynthia L., and Marilynn B. Brewer. 2005. "The Role of Exclusion in Maintaining Ingroup Inclusion." In *The Social Psychology of Inclusion and Exclusion,* edited by Dominic Abrams, Michael A. Hogg, and José M. Marques. New York: Psychology Press.

Pieper, Christopher, and Matt Henderson. 2017. "10 Reasons You Can't Be a Christian and Vote for Donald Trump." *Dallas News,* November 6. www.dallasnews.com/opinion/commentary/2016/02/29/pieper-and-henderson-10-reasons-you-cant-be-a-christian-and-vote-for-donald-trump (accessed January 11, 2018).

Portes, Alejandro, ed. 1996. *The New Second Generation.* New York: Russell Sage Foundation.

Portes, Alejandro, and Rubén G. Rumbaut. 2001. *Legacies: The Story of the Immigrant Second Generation.* Berkeley: University of California Press.

————. 2014. *Immigrant America: A Portrait.* 4th ed. Berkeley: University of California Press.

Putnam, Robert. 2010. "American Grace." Tanner Lectures on Human Values delivered at Princeton University, Princeton, N.J., October 27–28. http://tannerlectures.utah.edu/_documents/a-to-z/p/Putnam_10.pdf (accessed January 11, 2018).

Putnam, Robert D., and David E. Campbell. 2010. *American Grace: How Religion Divides and Unites Us.* New York: Simon & Schuster.

Ramakrishnan, Karthick. 2005. *Democracy in Immigrant America: Changing Demographics and Political Participation.* Palo Alto, Calif.: Stanford University Press.

Ramakrishnan, Karthick, Jane Junn, Taeku Lee, and Janelle Wong. 2012. 2008 National Asian American Survey (computer file). ICPSR31481-v2, Inter-university Consortium for Political and Social Research, Ann Arbor, Mich. (distributor). http://www.icpsr.umich.edu/icpsrweb/RCMD/studies/31481 (accessed January 11, 2018).

Ramakrishnan, Karthick, Janelle Wong, Jennifer Lee, and Taeku Lee. 2016. "Asian American Voices in the 2016 Election: Report on Registered Voters in the Fall 2016 National Asian American Survey." October 5. http://naasurvey.com/wp-content/uploads/2016/10/NAAS2016-Oct5-report.pdf (accessed January 11, 2018).

Ramírez, Ricardo. 2013. *Mobilizing Opportunities: The Evolving Latino Electorate and the Future of American Politics.* Charlottesville: University of Virginia Press.

Robbins, Joel. 2004. "The Globalization of Pentecostal and Charismatic Christianity." *Annual Review of Anthropology* 33(October 21): 117–43. http://www.annual reviews.org/doi/10.1146/annurev.anthro.32.061002.093421 (accessed January 11, 2018).

Rodriguez, Samuel. 2016. "Rev. Rodriguez Responds to GOP Platform." Letter to Honorable Paul Ryan, Speaker, U.S. House of Representatives. *Faith and Education Coalition.* http://www.faithandeducation.com/rev-rodriguez-responds-to-gop-platform (accessed January 11, 2018).

Roozen, David. 2013. "Negative Numbers: The Decline Narrative Reaches Evangelicals." *Christian Century,* December 3. https://www.christiancentury.org/article/2013-11/negative-numbers (accessed January 11, 2018).

Rouse, Stella M., Betina Cutaia Wilkinson, and James C. Garand. 2010. "Divided Loyalties? Understanding Variation in Latino Attitudes Toward Immigration." *Social Science Quarterly* 91(3): 856–82. doi:10.1111/j.1540-6237.2010.00723.x.

Ryrie, Alec. 2017. "The Weakness of the Religious Left: How Progressive Evangelicals Ceded Moral Authority to the Right Wing." *Salon,* April 9. http://www.salon.com/2017/04/09/the-weakness-of-the-religious-left-how-progressive-evangelicals-ceded-moral-authority-to-the-right-wing/ (accessed January 11, 2018).

Salguero, Gabriel. 2010. "An Open Letter to Governor Brewer of Arizona." *Sojourners,* April 22. https://sojo.net/articles/open-letter-governor-brewer-arizona (accessed January 11, 2018).

———. 2016. "Evangelicals Are Not a Monolith." *New York Times,* June 1. http://www.nytimes.com/roomfordebate/2016/03/07/what-does-it-mean-to-be-evangelical-today/evangelicals-are-not-a-monolith (accessed January 11, 2018).

Savidge, Martin. 2016. "Florida: The Swingiest Swing State in the U.S. Election." *CNN Politics,* August 9. http://www.cnn.com/2016/08/09/politics/election-2016-donald-trump-hillary-clinton-florida/index.html (accessed January 11, 2018).

Seidman, Irving. 1991. "A Structure for In-depth, Phenomenological Interviewing." In Seidman, *Interviewing as Qualitative Research: A Guide for Researchers in Education and the Social Sciences.* New York: Teachers College Press.

Sherkat, Darren E., Kylan Mattias De Vries, and Stacia Creek. 2010. "Race, Religion, and Opposition to Same-Sex Marriage." *Social Science Quarterly* 91(1): 80–98. doi:10.1111/j.1540-6237.2010.00682.x.

Showalter, Brandon. 2016. "Trump Should 'Heal the Hurt' Caused by 'Inflammatory' Rhetoric About Latinos, Samuel Rodriguez Says." *Christian Post,* May 10. http://www.christianpost.com/news/trump-heal-the-hurt-inflammatory-rhetoric-latino-hispanic-samuel-rodriguez-163656/ (accessed January 11, 2018).

Smidt, Corwin. 1987. "Evangelicals and the 1984 Election: Continuity or Change?" *American Politics Quarterly* 15(4): 419–44. doi:10.1177/1532673X8701500401.

———. 2007. "Evangelical and Mainline Protestants at the Turn of the Millennium: Taking Stock and Looking Forward." In *From Pews to Polling Places: Faith and Politics in the American Religious Mosaic,* edited by J. Matthew Wilson. Washington, D.C.: Georgetown University Press.

Smith, Buster G., and Byron Johnson. 2010. "The Liberalization of Young Evangelicals: A Research Note." *Journal for the Scientific Study of Religion* 49(2): 351–60. doi: 10.1111/j.1468-5906.2010.01514.x.

Smith, Christian. 2000. *Christian America? What Evangelicals Really Want.* Berkeley: University of California Press.

Smith, Christian, Michael Emerson, Sally Gallagher, Paul Kennedy, and David Sikkink. 1998. *American Evangelicalism: Embattled and Thriving.* Chicago: University of Chicago Press.

Smith, Gregory A. 2006. "Attitudes Toward Immigration: In the Pulpit and the Pew." Pew Research Center, Washington, D.C., April 25. http://www.pewresearch.org/2006/04/25/attitudes-toward-immigration-in-the-pulpit-and-the-pew/ (accessed January 11, 2018).

Smith, Gregory, and Jessica Martinez. 2016. "How the Faithful Voted: A Preliminary 2016 Analysis." Pew Research Center, Washington, D.C., November 9. http://pewresearch.org/fact-tank/2016/11/09/how-the-faithful-voted-a-preliminary-2016-analysis (accessed January 11, 2018).

Stafford, Tim. 2006. "The Call of Samuel." *Christianity Today,* September 1. http://www.christianitytoday.com/ct/2006/september/31.82.html (accessed January 11, 2018).

Stetzer, Ed. 2016. "In a Dramatic Shift, the American Church Is More Evangelical Than Ever." *Washington Post,* May 14. https://www.washingtonpost.com/news/acts-of-faith/wp/2015/05/14/in-a-dramatic-shift-the-american-church-is-more-evangelical-than-ever/ (accessed January 11, 2018).

Streeter, Kurt. 2014. "Spreading the Pentecostal Spirit." *Los Angeles Times,* February 2. www.latimes.com/local/la-me-latino-pentecostal-20140202-story.html (accessed January 11, 2018).

Strolovitch, Dara Z. 2007. *Affirmative Advocacy: Race, Class, and Gender in Interest Group Politics.* Chicago: University of Chicago Press.

Tajfel, Henri, ed. 1978. *Differentiation Between Social Groups: Studies in the Social Psychology of Intergroup Relations.* Vol. 14, *European Monographs in Social Psychology.* London: Academic Press.

Taylor, J. Benjamin, Sarah Allen Gershon, and Adrian D. Pantoja. 2014. "Christian America? Understanding the Link Between Churches, Attitudes, and 'Being American' Among Latino Immigrants." *Politics and Religion* 7(2): 339–65. doi:10.1017/S1755048314000042.

Templon, John. 2016. "How the Electoral College Favors White Voters." *BuzzFeed,* November 7. https://www.buzzfeed.com/johntemplon/how-the-electoral-college-screws-hispanic-and-asian-voters (accessed January 11, 2018).

Theiss-Morse, Elizabeth. 2009. *Who Counts as an American? The Boundaries of National Identity.* New York: Cambridge University Press.

Umaña-Taylor, Adriana J., Marcelo Diversi, and Mark A. Fine. 2002. "Ethnic Identity and Self-Esteem of Latino Adolescents: Distinctions Among the Latino Populations." *Journal of Adolescent Research* 17(3): 303–27.

Valenzuela, Ali Adam. 2014. "Tending the Flock: Latino Religious Commitments and Political Preferences." *Political Research Quarterly* 67(4). doi:10.1177/1065912914543835.

Wadsworth, Nancy D. 2008. "Reconciling Fractures: The Intersection of Race and Religion in United States Political Development." In *Race and American Political Development,* edited by Joseph E. Lowndes, Julie Novkov, and Dorian T. Warren. New York: Routledge.

Wallace, Sophia J. 2012. "It's Complicated: Latinos, President Obama, and the 2012 Election." *Social Science Quarterly* 93(5): 1360–83. doi:10.1111/j.1540-6237.2012.00922.x.

Washington Post Opinions Staff. 2016. "A Transcript of Donald Trump's Meeting with the *Washington Post* Editorial Board." *Washington Post,* March 21. https://www.washingtonpost.com/blogs/post-partisan/wp/2016/03/21/a-transcript-of-donald-trumps-meeting-with-the-washington-post-editorial-board/ (accessed January 11, 2018).

Watanabe, Teresa, and Hector Becerra. 2006. "500,000 Pack Streets to Protest Immigration Bills." *Los Angeles Times,* March 26. http://articles.latimes.com/2006/mar/26/local/me-immig26, A-25 (accessed January 11, 2018).

Wilcox, Clyde, and Ted Jelen. 1990. "Evangelicals and Political Tolerance." *American Politics Quarterly* 18(1): 25–46. doi:10.1177/1532673X9001800102.

Wilcox, Clyde, and Carin Robinson. 2010. *Onward Christian Soldiers? The Religious Right in American Politics.* 4th ed. Boulder, Colo.: Westview Press.

Wilson, J. Matthew. 2007. *From Pews to Polling Places: Faith and Politics in the American Religious Mosaic.* Washington, D.C.: Georgetown University Press.

Withrow, Brandon. 2016. "They Have Faith Their Church Will Change." *Daily Beast,* September 25. http://www.thedailybeast.com/they-have-faith-their-church-will-change (accessed January 11, 2018).

Wong, Janelle. 2006. *Democracy's Promise: Immigrants and American Civic Institutions.* Ann Arbor: University of Michigan Press.

———. 2014. "Democrat, Republican, or Born-Again? How Asian American Evangelicals Disrupt Traditional Political Coalitions." Paper presented at the Annual Meeting of the Association of Asian American Studies, San Francisco, April 16–19.

———. 2015. "The Role of Born-Again Identity on the Political Attitudes of Whites, Blacks, Latinos, and Asian Americans." *Politics and Religion* 8(4): 641–78.

Wong, Janelle S., S. Karthick Ramakrishnan, Taeku Lee, and Jane Junn. 2011. *Asian American Political Participation: Emerging Constituents and Their Political Identities.* New York: Russell Sage Foundation.

Wuthnow, Robert. 1989. *The Struggle for America's Soul: Evangelicals, Liberals, and Secularism.* Grand Rapids, Mich.: Eerdmans.

Young, Neil J. 2015. *We Gather Together: The Religious Right and the Problem of Interfaith Politics.* New York: Oxford University Press.

Zhou, Min, Anthony C. Ocampo, and J. V. Gatewood. 2016. "Contemporary Asian America: Immigration, Demographic Transformation, and Ethnic Formation." In *Contemporary Asian America: A Multidisciplinary Reader* (3rd edition), edited by Min Zhou and Anthony C. Ocampo. New York: New York University Press.

Zogby, John. 2016. "Young Evangelicals Cheer Obama—For Now." *Forbes,* January 22. http://www.forbes.com/2009/01/21/evangelicals-polls-obama-oped-cx_jz_0122zogby.html (accessed January 11, 2018).

INDEX

Boldface numbers refer to figures and tables.